Miracles Around Us

Ron Rhodes

HARVEST HOUSE PUBLISHERS
Eugene, Oregon 97402

Cover by Terry Dugan Design, Minneapolis, Minnesota

MIRACLES AROUND US
Copyright © 2000 by Ron Rhodes
Published by Harvest House Publishers
Eugene, Oregon 97402

Library of Congress Cataloging-in-Publication Data

Rhodes, Ron
    Miracles around us / Ron Rhodes.
        p. cm.
    Includes bibliographical references.
    ISBN: 0-7369-0211-2
    1. Miracles. I. Title.
    BT97.2 .R45 2000
    231.7'8—dc21   00-027605

Printed in the United States of America.

00 01 02 03 04 05 06 07 08 09 / BC-BG / 10 9 8 7 6 5 4 3 2 1

In loving memory of Thomas Paul Rhodes

Acknowledgments

With every passing year, my appreciation only grows for the wonderful family God has given me. Kerri, David, and Kylie—please accept my heartfelt thanks for your sacrificial commitment to my work of ministry! I couldn't do it without you.

Most important, I want to acknowledge the one true God who has sent so many providential miracles my way through the years. It is before Him that I humbly bow in gratitude.

I will meditate on all your works and
consider all your mighty deeds.
Your ways, O God, are holy.
What god is so great as our God?
You are the God who performs miracles;
you display your power among the peoples.

— Psalm 77:12-14

Contents

~

ONE

When Heaven Touches Earth

It was a Wednesday afternoon. Shrouded in a dense fog, a large steamer edged slowly forward off the coast of Newfoundland, its foghorn crying out somber notes of warning. The captain—near exhaustion from lack of sleep—was startled by a gentle tap on his shoulder. He turned and found himself face-to-face with an old man in his late seventies.[1]

The old man said, "Captain, I have come to tell you that I must be in Quebec on Saturday afternoon."

The captain pondered for a moment and then snorted: "Impossible."

"Very well," the old man responded, "if your ship can't take me, God will find some other means to take me. I have never broken an engagement in 57 years."

Lifting his weary hands in a gesture of despair, the captain replied, "I would help if I could—but I am helpless."

Undaunted, the old man suggested, "Let's go down to the chart room and pray." The captain raised his eyebrows in utter disbelief, looking at the old man as if he had just escaped from a lunatic asylum.

"Do you know how dense the fog is?" the captain demanded.

The old man responded, "No. My eye is not on the thickness of the fog but on the living God who controls every circumstance of my life."

Against his better judgment, the captain accompanied the old man to the chart room and kneeled with him in prayer. With simple words a child might use, the old man prayed: "O Lord, if it is consistent with Thy will, please remove this fog in five minutes. Thou knowest the engagement Thou didst make for me in Quebec on Saturday. I believe it is Thy will."

The captain, a nominal Christian at best, thought it wise to humor the old man and recite a short prayer. But before he was able to utter a single word, he felt a tap on his shoulder. The old man requested, "Don't pray, because you do not believe; and as I believe God has already answered, there is no need for you to pray." The captain's mouth dropped open.

Then the old man explained, "Captain, I have known my Lord for 57 years, and there has never been a single day that I have failed to gain an audience with the King. Get up, captain, and open the door, and you will find the fog is gone."

The captain did as he was requested and was astonished to find the fog had indeed disappeared.

The captain later testified that his encounter with the aged George Müller completely revolutionized his Christian life. He had seen with his own eyes that Müller's God was the true and living God of the Bible. He had seen incredible power flow from a frail old man—a power rooted in simple childlike faith in a miraculous God.

On another occasion, Müller had witnessed God's provision for the many orphans under his care—too many, in fact, for one man to financially support without God's intervention. At his orphanage one morning the tables were all set for breakfast, but the cupboard was completely bare. There was no food! And there was no money![2]

The children were all standing around, waiting for their breakfasts. Mr. Müller said to them, "Children, you know we must be in time for school." He then lifted his head and prayed, "Dear Father, we thank Thee for what Thou art going to give us to eat."

Almost immediately after this, there was a knock at the door. It was a local baker, who said, "Mr. Müller, I could not sleep last night. Somehow I felt you didn't have any bread for breakfast, and the Lord wanted me to send you some. So I got up at 2:00 A.M. and baked some fresh bread, and here it is." Mr. Müller humbly thanked the baker and then offered praise to God for providing so miraculously for him and the orphans.

Moments later there was a second knock at the door. It was the local milkman, whose milk wagon had just broken down in front of Müller's orphanage. He offered all his milk to Müller and the orphans so he could have his wagon hauled to the nearest repair shop.

Were these occurrences in Müller's life mere coincidences? Many in our secular world would say so. Yet Müller knew otherwise. He believed in a God who is actively involved in the lives of His children. He believed in a God who is sovereign over human affairs.

A Seminary Rescued

I spent seven wonderful years at Dallas Theological Seminary, first obtaining my Master of Theology degree in 1983, and then my Doctor of Theology degree in 1986. During those years, God prepared me for a life of ministry. I will always be thankful to God for the education I received there.

Early in its history, Dallas Theological Seminary found itself near bankruptcy. And the way God financially rescued the seminary truly has the ring of the supernatural.

The seminary had been founded in 1924. It wasn't long after the founding that the money seemed to run out. Various creditors were all set to foreclose at noon on a particular day. Yet the founders of the school were confident Dallas Theological Seminary was a work ordained by God, and God would somehow make provisions for the survival of the seminary. So despite the tremendous odds against the school, the founders met in the president's office to plead before God.

In the prayer meeting, it came time for the eminent scholar Dr. Harry Ironside to pray. He said, "Lord, we know that the cattle on a thousand hills are thine. Please sell some of them and send us the money."

While they were all still in the midst of praying to God, a tall Texan came into the business office and said, "I just sold two carloads of cattle in Fort Worth. I've been trying to make a business deal go through, and it won't work, and I feel that God is compelling me to give this money to the seminary. I don't know if you need it or not, but here's the check."

The secretary in the business office took the check and rushed over to the door of the room where the prayer meeting was taking place, and she knocked gently. After a few moments, the door opened, and Dr. Lewis Sperry Chafer, president of the seminary, took the check out of her hand—and it was for the exact amount of the seminary's debt. When he looked at the signature, he recognized the name of the cattle rancher. Turning to Dr. Ironside, he said, "Harry, God sold the cattle."[3]

Coincidence? Many in our secular world would say so. But the founders of Dallas Theological Seminary knew otherwise.

They believed in a God who is in sovereign control over the world and answers the prayers of His children.

Tuberculosis Healed

Elisabeth Elliot was born of missionary parents in Brussels, Belgium. She too became involved in missionary work, alongside her husband, Jim Elliot. After spending a year in Ecuador, engaging in missionary work among the Auca Indians, she married her college friend Jim in Quito. Following her husband's death at the hands of the Aucas, whom he had been attempting to reach for Christ, she ended up making successful contact with them. Through her work of Bible translation, she carried on Jim's goal of bringing the gospel to primitive tribes.[4]

Prior to their marriage, Jim and Elisabeth had faced a serious test of faith. There came a point when Elisabeth developed some threatening health problems, so she went to the doctor. Elisabeth recalls:

> We were informed that, according to X-rays, I had an active case of tuberculosis. Knowing as well as Jim did that he was called to the Indians of the jungle, I felt that this news spelled the cancellation of our marriage plans, for even if I should recover, life in the jungle would not be recommended for me. Jim's attitude, however, was unchanged.[5]

Tuberculosis is a serious disease. It is an acute bacterial infection that primarily attacks the lungs. Symptoms include coughing, chest pain, shortness of breath, loss of appetite, weight loss, fever, chills, and fatigue. Half of all untreated cases are fatal. Both Jim and Elisabeth knew the seriousness of what they faced.

Yet Jim would later speak in his personal journal of his faith in God in the midst of this trial:

If I had any plans, they are not changed. I will marry her in God's time, and it will be the very best for us, even if it means waiting years. God has not led us this far to frustrate us or turn us back, and He knows all about how to handle TB. I don't know what this means. I only know that God is in the generation of the righteous, and guides their steps aright. Beyond His counsel and will there is no going. I am there now, and want nothing more.[6]

Jim modeled for all around him an attitude of complete faith in the midst of the storm. And his faith was rewarded with divine intervention in Elisabeth's life. As Elisabeth put it, "A week's further tests showed nothing whatever wrong with my lungs."[7]

Sally's Sorrow Turned to Joy

Sally, a woman who attends my church, could not restrain her tears as she poured out her heart to Pastor Dave. After a series of medical tests, Sally's doctor had called to inform her the baby she was expecting would be born with Down's syndrome. Pastor Dave shared Sally's grief at the news. He vowed to help Sally and her husband Jim in any way he could.[8]

The following day Pastor Dave decided to send Sally and Jim a postcard with a word of encouragement. On the card, Dave assured them of how much God loved them and their soon-to-be-born little baby.

The postcard ended up being delivered to a wrong address a number of miles from Sally and Jim's house. Sue—who lived at the house the card was mistakenly delivered to—decided to take the postcard to Sally personally.

When Sally opened the door, Sue said, "This card from your pastor was delivered to my house by mistake. I wanted to come by and deliver the card personally because I too have a child with Down's Syndrome, and I want to help you through this if you'll let me. God has shown me so much I would like to share with you."

Did the God of all comfort "reroute" the mail to Sue's house? We can't know for certain, but it surely seems a good possibility. While the world would tell us this was just a freak accident, I see supernatural intervention written all over this event.

Confounding an Unbelieving Professor

Jodie Berndt, a former producer for the Christian Broadcasting Network, speaks of a friend who had an interesting encounter in a secular philosophy class at a Virginia university. Here's what happened:

> Every year the philosophy professor began the first day of his class with the same forceful questions. "Who here believes in God? Is God all-powerful? Can He do miracles? Does He want to be known?"
>
> Scanning his audience of eager minds, the professor held up a glass jar. "I'm holding this jar," he said. "Is there anyone here who will pray to God so that the jar will not break when I drop it?"
>
> The challenge hung in the air. "Every year, for seventeen years, we've tried this experiment—and the jar always breaks. It breaks because God is not real or operative in today's world. Now, is there anyone here who wants to pray?"
>
> Just as the professor had expected, the room was silent. Suddenly, though, one boy spoke up. His tone was quiet but firm. "I'll pray that prayer," he said.
>
> The professor was taken aback. No one, it seemed, had ever accepted his challenge. "Okay," he said. "What should we do? Should we bow our heads?"

"You can do whatever you like," the boy said simply. And then he prayed. "God, I pray You would honor Your name today. Amen."

The anticipation was palpable as the professor lifted the jar. He released his hold—and the jar fell to the ground, struck the teacher's foot, and rolled to one side, intact.

The room erupted as students stood and stretched to see what had happened. There were some in the front row who swore they saw the jar's path curve inward as it fell. Others, however, put the matter down to a poorly executed drop by the eager professor.[9]

Again, we ask, was this a mere coincidence? I do not have any indisputable proof that God was involved. The world would tell us this was a freak incident. But the boy in the class is a believer in the fact that God not only exists but is active in the world today, despite the allegations of the unbelieving professor.

Rescued En Route to China

Hudson Taylor's father, James, had always been intrigued by China. He was fascinated to think that even though great empires like Persia, Greece, and Rome had risen and fallen, the Chinese empire had remained. Early in 1832, James knelt beside his young wife Amelia and prayed, "Dear God, if You should give us a son, grant that he may work for You in China."[10]

When their child was born on May 21, 1832, James and Amelia named him James Hudson Taylor. It is highly telling of young Hudson's sense of direction in life that as a boy he would sometimes blurt out, "When I am a man, I mean to be a missionary and go to China." This was the case even though his parents were not to tell him of their prayer for some years.[11]

Just after his twenty-first birthday, young Hudson Taylor found himself en route to China on a small sailing-ship, the *Dumfries,* from Liverpool. As they were sailing to the north of New Guinea, there would be breezes after sundown that would last until dawn, but during the daytime they were frequently becalmed.

On one particular day, this caused great concern to the captain of the small ship because some strong undercurrents were carrying them straight toward some sunken reefs. This could spell disaster for everyone aboard. *How they needed a strong breeze to launch them out of that area!*

The captain tried a number of maneuvers, but it was no use. Nothing seemed to work. But then young Hudson Taylor piped up and said, "There is one thing we have not done yet—we have not prayed."

There were three other Christians aboard the ship, and Hudson suggested they all go to their cabins to pray. They did so. After only a few minutes, Hudson felt an assurance that God would deliver the ship. He promptly went to the deck and requested that the first officer (an unbeliever) set the sail so it would catch the approaching wind. That didn't go over too well. The man was utterly flabbergasted that anyone—especially a *religious nut!*—would have the gall to make such a suggestion to an experienced seaman like him. But Hudson persisted, affirming to the man that God would indeed send a wind.

With no time to lose, the first officer—against what he considered to be his better judgment—gave the order, and the men jumped to obey. The captain then rushed up on deck to find out what was going on, and right before the eyes of everyone present, the sails filled with wind, and the ship sped away from the reef in safety.[12]

A coincidence? No one can actually "prove" it was God who arranged the wind to arrive just in the nick of time. But Hudson and his friends were certain of God's involvement. They believed in a God who truly answers prayer and involves Himself in the lives of those committed to Him.

Rescued on the Missionary Field

Reverend John G. Paton was a missionary in the New Hebrides Islands (now Vanuatu) in the southwest Pacific.[13] According to his testimony, his mission headquarters were surrounded one night by hostile natives, who apparently intended to burn the buildings to the ground and put Paton and his wife to death.

The Patons turned to God, throwing themselves on His mercy. They asked Him to deliver them. They prayed throughout the night. And when the first rays of sunlight came the next morning, the Patons were utterly amazed to see that the hostile natives had left.

About a year later, the chief of the tribe of hostile natives became a Christian. And when Paton asked the chief why the tribe had refrained from burning down the headquarters on that fateful night, to Paton's surprise the chief asked, "Who were all those men you had there with you?" Paton answered, "There were no men there; just my wife and I."

The chief then informed Paton that he and his men had seen hundreds of men standing guard outside the headquarters, all dressed in shining garments with swords drawn. They had literally encircled the headquarters, and the tribe had not dared to attack.

It was then Paton realized that God had dispatched His angels to guard him and his wife. As Psalm 34:7 tells us, "The angel of the LORD encamps around those who fear him, and he delivers them." Moreover, "He will command his angels concerning you to guard you in all your ways" (Psalm 91:11).

Paton's testimony sounds remarkably similar to the story of Elisha in 2 Kings 6:15-17. In this account Elisha and his servant were utterly surrounded by hostile forces. But they were not alone:

> When the servant of the man of God got up and went out early the next morning, an army with horses and chariots had surrounded the city. "Oh, my lord, what shall we do?" the servant asked.
>
> "Don't be afraid," the prophet answered. "Those who are with us are more than those who are with them."
>
> And Elisha prayed, "O LORD, open his eyes so he may see." Then the LORD opened the servant's eyes, and he looked and saw the hills full of horses and chariots of fire all around Elisha.

Just as the God of miracles rescued Elisha and his servant, so He rescued Reverend Paton and his wife. The world would say all this is nonsense. But Reverend Paton knows better.

A Little Boy's Heart Encouraged

As I write this chapter, my 12-year-old boy David has been having verbal abuse heaped on him by a boy in the neighborhood who believes in evolution. This boy has been taking every opportunity to berate David over his belief in creationism. I've been concerned about this because I am aware of how easy it is for a little boy to get his heart bruised.

Besides helping David beef up his defense of creationism, I prayed specifically during my devotional time this morning that God would use someone *this very day* to speak an encouraging word to David out of the blue. I prayed that David, before the day was over, would be on the receiving end of an unexpected act of kindness that would bring cheer to his heart.

Later in the afternoon, as all of us were congregated in the family room, my 10-year-old daughter Kylie—completely unaware of my earlier prayer—handed David a note she had just written about him. Here are her exact words:

> David is cool, because whenever I'm in a bad situation, he sticks up for me. He is also helpful because he helps clean the house. He is a great kid. I love him.

I wish I had had a video camera to capture how David's face lit up as he read those words. *What a perfect answer to prayer!* I felt like giving God a standing ovation right then and there.

A Thankful Wife

Chuck Swindoll, in his book *The Finishing Touch,* shares a powerful true story that shows God's providential timing in the affairs of His children:

> In September, Terry Shafer was strolling the shops in Moline, Illinois. She knew exactly what she wanted to get her husband, David, for Christmas, but she realized it might be too expensive. A little shop on Fifth attracted her attention, so she stepped inside. Her eyes darted toward the corner display. "That's it!" she smiled as she nodded with pleasure. "How much?" she asked the shopkeeper.
>
> "Only $127.50."
>
> Her smile faded into disappointment as she realized David's salary couldn't stand such a jolt. He was feeding and clothing the family on a policeman's wage. It was out of the question. Yet she hated to give up without a try, so she applied a little persistence.

"Uh, what about putting this aside for me? Maybe I could pay a little each week, then pick it up a few days before Christmas?"

"No," the merchant said, "I won't do that." Then he smiled. "I'll gift-wrap it right now. You can take it with you and pay me later," he said.

Terry was elated. She agreed to pay so much every week, then thanked and thanked the man as she left, explaining how delighted her husband would be.

"Oh, that's nothing at all," the shopkeeper answered, not realizing the significant role his generosity would play in the days ahead.

Then came Saturday, October 1. Patrolman David Shafer, working the night shift, got a call in his squad car. A drugstore robbery was in progress. David reacted instantly, arriving on scene just in time to see the suspect speed away. With siren screaming and lights flashing, he followed in hot pursuit. Three blocks later the getaway vehicle suddenly pulled over and stopped. The driver didn't move. David carefully approached the suspect with his weapon drawn. When he was only three feet from the driver's door, two things happened in a split second. The door flew open as the thief produced a 45-caliber pistol and fired at David's abdomen.

At seven o'clock that morning, a patrolman came to the door of the Shafer home. Calmly and with great care, he told Terry what had happened.

Her husband had been pursuing a robbery suspect. There had been gunfire. David was hit. Shot at pointblank range.

Stunned, Terry thought how glad she was that she had not waited until Christmas to give her husband his present. How grateful she was that the shopkeeper had been willing to let her pay for it later. Otherwise, David would have surely died. Instead, he was now in the hospital—not with a gunshot wound, but with only a bad bruise.

You see, David was wearing the gift of life Terry could not wait to give—his brand-new bulletproof vest.[14]

This is yet another one of those events that the world would call a lucky coincidence—or perhaps just "good timing." But David's wife Terry sees the hand of God at work here. In her mind, God in *His perfect providential timing* made miraculous provision for keeping her husband alive.

The Miracle of Forgiveness

Corrie ten Boom tells the following true story in her book, *The Hiding Place:*

> It was at a church service in Munich that I saw him, the former S.S. man [Nazi policeman] who had stood guard at the shower room door in the processing center at Ravensbruck. He was the first of our actual jailers that I had seen since that time. And suddenly it was all there—the roomful of mocking men, the heaps of clothing, Betsie's pain-blanched face.
>
> He came up to me as the church was emptying, beaming and bowing. "How grateful I am for your message, Fräulein," he said. "To think that, as you say, He has washed my sins away!"
>
> His hand was thrust out to shake mine. And I, who had preached so often to the people in Bloemendaal the need to forgive, kept my hand at my side.
>
> Even as the angry, vengeful thoughts boiled through me, I saw the sin of them. Jesus Christ had died for this man; was I going to ask for more? Lord Jesus, I prayed, forgive me and help me to forgive him.

I tried to smile, I struggled to raise my hand. I could not. I felt nothing, not the slightest spark of warmth or charity. And so again I breathed a silent prayer. Jesus, I cannot forgive him. Give me Your forgiveness.

As I took his hand the most incredible thing happened. From my shoulder along my arm and through my hand, a current seemed to pass from me to him, while into my heart sprang a love for this stranger that almost overwhelmed me.

And so I discovered that it is not on our forgiveness any more than on our goodness that the world's healing hinges, but on His. When He tells us to love our enemies, He gives, along with the command, the love itself.[15]

Here is a woman who had suffered *immensely* at the hands of her S.S. captors. The scarring on her heart must have been deep and painful. Yet, through Christ, Corrie ten Boom was able to truly forgive and reach out to this man. Just as the supernatural power of Christ has brought physical healing to so many people, so the supernatural power of Christ can also bring emotional healing.

Were These True Miracles?

Were the events described above true miracles of God? Or were they something else? If they were not miracles in the sense that the *Bible* defines miracles, then what do we call them? Are they "providential acts of God"? What should be our attitude toward such events? And if *our* "miracle" doesn't come, what are we to conclude about God? Does He still love us and care for us?

These are some of the questions I will deal with in the pages that follow. And as we examine these and other issues, the governing source of truth will not be human experience, television shows, magazines, or newspapers, but rather the pages of Scripture—our *only* reliable barometer of truth.

At the outset, I want to call your attention to the fact that this book has been named purposefully *Miracles Around Us: How to Recognize God at Work Today*. Frankly, we are living in strange times. There are all kinds of claims out there—by Christians *and* those of a variety of different religions—regarding the issue of miracles. Hence, the question of "how to recognize God at work today" is an important one.

On the one hand, God *truly is* at work today in our midst. (I think the true stories above bear this out.) On the other hand, many things today that are claimed to be miracles of God *are not of God at all* but are rooted in another source (natural *or* supernatural)—perhaps even in human deception. And some things Christians call "miracles" today are not really miracles *in the sense that the Bible defines them.*

So, we need a good dose of discernment on this issue. Toward that end, you will find at the end of some chapters a box containing three or four "Points to Ponder." These are intended to be succinct principles of discernment that will assist you in recognizing *what is* of God and *what is not* of God concerning claims about miracles in our day. Let it be our goal to correctly handle the Word of Truth (2 Timothy 2:15).

~

Two

The Popularity
of Miracles

There was a time when miracles were relegated mainly to Sunday school and perhaps an occasional sermon. But not anymore. Miracles have infiltrated the popular culture—big time! Indeed, belief in miracles is soaring across the religious spectrum in America from mainline Christians to New Agers to Word-Faith proponents to the cultic Mind Sciences. Miracles seem to be everywhere these days. As one rabbi put it, "Miracles have become trendy, with numerous television shows, books, and songs on the phenomenon."[1]

In the last few years, miracles have moved from the inner halls of churches to feature articles in today's biggest magazines:

- *Life* magazine featured an article titled, "Miracles, USA—The Influence of Miraculous Happenings in Everyday Life."

- *Time* magazine published the article, "The Message of Miracles: Religious Controversy Over Validity of Miracles."

- *U.S. News and World Report* published the article, "The History of Miracles."

- *Redbook* magazine featured the article, "Do You Believe in Miracles?"

- *Good Housekeeping,* too, ran an article titled, "Do You Believe in Miracles?"

A phenomenal number of books on miracles have also been published in recent years. Just a few titles I came across in a visit to a bookstore include *Celebration of Miracles; Miracles Are Heaven Sent; Small Miracles: Extraordinary Stories of Ordinary People Touched by God; Miracles of the Saints;* and *Miracles Happen When You Pray.* There are virtually hundreds of others to choose from.

Miracles are certainly popular on television. One show that seems to have touched a nerve with the American public is a one-hour weekly series focusing on heartwarming, uplifting real-life stories of miraculous occurrences that airs on PAX-TV. The show is called *It's a Miracle,* and is hosted by Richard Thomas and Nia Peeples. It features alleged true-life stories from viewers about miraculous events that have happened to them or their families.[2] A press release for the show says, "Each week the show features unbelievable stories in which everyday lives are changed by incredible events that occur which cannot be explained except by the influence of divine intervention."[3] The show "inspires viewers with amazing human interest stories that tug at your heart." It is broadcast on more than 100 television stations across the country.[4]

As I write, one of the most popular movies in America is *The Green Mile,* starring Tom Hanks. The central figure in the movie is a death-row inmate who has astonishing miraculous powers. He is portrayed as instantly healing one person of a severe bladder infection, another person of cancer in advanced stages, and bringing a crushed and bloodied mouse back to life. This person's miraculous abilities were said to have come from God. But the "miracles" performed by this person bear more resemblance to "New-Ageish" psychic phenomena than biblical miracles.

Another blockbuster movie with its fair share of miracles is *The Prince of Egypt*. This animated movie focuses on the miracles of Moses in the Exodus account, and the theme song of the movie assures us: "There can be miracles when you believe...."

Why so many books, magazine articles, television shows, and movies on miracles? The reason is simple: *A huge portion of the American public believes in miracles.* There is an immense market for miracles in this country.

In fact, pollster George Barna found that "most people take the Bible at face value when it comes to the descriptions of the miracles that took place. Three out of four adults (73%) believe that all of the miracles described in the Bible actually took place."[5]

In keeping with this, when a Gallup poll asked in 1988 if people believed miracles are still performed today by the power of God, 51 percent of those polled said they agreed completely. Only 6 percent said they didn't believe. When asked the same question in 1994, *79 percent* reported they believed in miracles.[6] That's a *28-percent* jump in just six years.

The following year (1995), a national survey indicated that 80 percent of all Americans believe in the miraculous.[7] A different poll conducted by the respected *Orange County Register,* one of California's leading daily newspapers, and based on almost 600 responses, indicated that 87 percent of those surveyed believe in miracles.[8] As I write (early in the year 2000), the polls continue to indicate a strong belief in the miraculous.

The demographic breakdown of the polls indicates that people *in all categories* believe in miracles. Newspaper columnist Tom Sheridan alerts us to the fact that

> in Gallup's polling, the highest numbers of miracle believers—84 percent—came from "baby boomers," those aged 30 to 49, but other age groups were represented only marginally less. Gender, race, region, education, and even household income do not greatly affect the conviction that miracles are a valid and important part of our world. Nor is there any statistical difference in belief between Protestant denominations and Roman Catholics. It's true that slightly more women than men believe, and Gallup reports that those for whom religion is important are twice as likely to recognize miracles.[9]

What all this means in a nutshell is that there is a huge, huge segment of the American population that believes in miracles. For some reason, miracles have struck a nerve with people today.

Understanding Today's Miracle Craze

The question that naturally comes to mind is, *Why* are miracles so popular in twentieth-century America?

Of course, Christians are excited about miracles because they fit with biblical doctrine—and their interest in miracles reflects their *greater* interest in Scripture and the supernatural miracle-working God of which Scripture speaks. Other people, however, have become excited about miracles because they have bought into some pretty strange ideas about this phenomenon. (I'll demonstrate this later in the book.) Cultural observers have suggested at least eight reasons (some closely related to each other) for the increasing popularity of miracles:

part here

1. People are more open about such things today. Miracles used to be a "hush-hush" topic ("people might think you're crazy"), but no more. In an article entitled "Why More People Believe in God and Miracles," we are told that people have taken God and miracles "out of the closet." People are now more willing to talk about such things. "People used to be afraid to say 'the voice' told me because they thought others would call them crazy. But as soon as one person said, 'God spoke to me,' there was the *Amen* corner. People are saying it more openly."[10] One might even say that it's "in" to talk about miraculous phenomena these days. Turn on your favorite television talk show, and it wouldn't be unusual to hear someone touch on some aspect of the miraculous.

2. People are tired of the materialism and secularism of Western society. Popular writer Sophy Burnham says, "I think Americans in the '80s became weary of 20 years of materialism. We were spiritually starved and hungry for some hope and inspiration."[11] Miracles give us that hope and inspiration. Eileen Elias Freeman, another best-selling author, says there's a hunger out there for accounts of miracles. "Materialism hasn't made us happy," she explains. "Money and power haven't solved our problems. So now people are looking for spiritual answers."[12] Indeed, "we've come through a very materialistic period in this country. People are searching for a deeper spirituality."[13]

Many who have cast in their lot with the miraculous say it has become easier to believe in such phenomena as we see evidence that high technology is limited in its ability to solve societal ills. Many say high technology has not taken us where we need to be, and hence there is more interest in spiritual things (like the miraculous). Rabbi Joshua Finkelstein commented that television shows like *Touched by an Angel* are doing well because "people feel this is a phenomenon in their life…. Maybe this is a reaction to the scientific and technological revolution. People realize that not all the answers are on a microchip and are turning toward other areas."[14]

3. Today's "spiritual awakening" has naturally led to a belief in miracles. Many people have seen firsthand what a life without God is like—and they've seen what solutions to life's problems without involvement of the divine are like. Now that they've committed their lives to God (or some kind of divinity), belief in miracles is a natural part of their new spiritual worldview.[15] An important factor I want to note here is that the "spiritual awakening" I speak of is not limited to Christianity. Certainly many people *have* awakened to Christianity, and we can be thankful for that. But many others today have turned to one of the many new religions that have blossomed on American soil.

Of course, America has always been fertile soil for the growth of new religions. Historian Sydney Ahlstrom says "American civilization from the beginning and in each passing century has been continuously marked by extraordinary religious fertility, and continues to exhibit this propensity to the present day."[16]

Since the 1960s, there has been a virtual explosion of religious pluralism in this country. This explosion has led one observer to comment, "More than ever ours is a pluralistic society in which Christianity is no longer a consensus but just another option in a whole cafeteria of religious choices."[17] New religions are proliferating in America at a geometric pace. As columnist Pat Buchanan noted, "Americans of left and right no longer share the same religion, the same values, the same codes of morality; we only inhabit the same piece of land."[18]

Accompanying this explosion of new religions has been a belief in miracles—and these various religions teach a variety of things about miracles. For instance, among New Agers one can purchase the three-volume tome *A Course in Miracles* and join one of over 1000 study groups in the United States that meet weekly to learn how to create metaphysical miracles based on this course. Those involved in the Mind Sciences (such as Religious Science or the Unity School of Christianity) will tell you that the secret of miracles is in the mind. Indeed, by using the right kind of thoughts, one can heal illnesses and create health and wealth. (Word-Faith proponents believe the same thing.) Psychic healers use various occultic methods to bring about alleged healings of people. Witches and neopagans hold that the miraculous is rooted in Mother Earth or the Mother Goddess. As we will see throughout the rest of this book, these religions are not setting forth *true* miracles of God but rather counterfeit miracles.

4. People are in need of reassurance today. An article in *Redbook* magazine suggests interest in miracles is a natural result of the upsurge of anxiety in our times. "Life is so stressful, the future is so uncertain. People are hungry for a reassuring sign that God still cares for his children on earth."[19]

Our world often seems threatening and out of control. The family unit is dissolving; crime is skyrocketing; terrorism is spreading at an unprecedented pace; more and more nations have attained nuclear capability; governments are corrupt; and natural disasters are claiming tens of thousands of lives. There is a lot to worry about these days. For many people, the belief that God still does miracles leads to a sense of security. It shows that God is still involved in the affairs of humankind.

5. *People have personal needs and desire help from a "higher source."* The current polls indicate that Americans most frequently seek God's help (including His miracles) when facing a challenge (92 percent), when dealing with a personal problem (80 percent), and when frightened (79 percent).[20] There are a great many people out there who perceive that they *really need* a personal miracle.

A pastor I came across in my reading said "more people are believing in God and miracles because man needs help from a higher source when it comes to handling trials and tribulations." Indeed, in our society an increasing number of people are realizing that to get help with some of the severe problems they face, they need to go to a source with abilities greater than ours. "People are learning that when they come to God sincerely, He will be able to perform miracles. He's a miracle-working God. He's able to do what the Bible says He can do."[21] So—many people would say that it's *not just* the problems out there in the world that have made people more open to the miraculous, it's also the problems in our own little spheres of existence—*our lives*—that cause us to be open to such things.

6. *Our natural solutions often fail, so we need supernatural help.* Closely related to the above, some people believe

because our finite, man-made *(natural)* solutions to the problems we face have failed, we need *supernatural* help from beyond. One article I came across noted: "This is the most unstable time in our culture. We are living in desperate times where people are going to believe in things they can't see because they can't trust the things they can see...Miracles happen where natural resources end. One will walk into the realm of miracles when all natural resources have been exhausted."[22] People today are yearning for *transcendent* help—help above and beyond what we are capable of in ourselves. Hence the yearning for miracles.

7. *People are sick and need healing.* Western medicine, despite its many advances through the years, has still failed to cure some of the most devastating diseases that plague our society. Many people are dying of cancer, heart disease, AIDS, various organ failures, and much more. Understandably, no one *wants* to die. If there's even a remote possibility that one could be miraculously cured, then that cure is something that should be pursued with fervor. Hence, many today are seeking miracles. A *Christianity Today* article reported:

> Our own science-dominated century has found little place for miracles. *Until now.* Suddenly, *Time* and other popular magazines are publishing cover stories on documented miracles of healing. News flash: Surgery patients recover faster when prayed for! It is a classic American turnabout. People who could never swallow the miracles in the Bible now show an intense interest in the potential for miracles to help them.[23]

8. *The media has heavily promoted belief in miracles.* Who would dare deny that the media has played a significant role in the increasing popularity of miracles? Not only are there television shows such as *It's a Miracle,* hosted by the popular Richard Thomas, but as one "channel-surfs" at night, one is bound to come across the likes of Benny Hinn and other faith healers, who are portrayed healing all kinds of incurable ailments. [I'll talk more about the Word-Faith movement later in the book.] As noted earlier, there is also a plethora of books, magazine articles, and even movies that have contributed to the miracle mania in our culture.

For these and perhaps many other reasons, miracles have never been more popular in Western society. The problem is, though, that alot of what is called "miraculous" in our culture is not *truly* miraculous at all. And even many of the things that *do* have the appearance of the supernatural at work are not necessarily rooted in the supernatural work of God. The devil is alive and well, and he is busy producing his supernatural counterfeits. In view of the present confusion, I will proceed in the next chapter to define what a miracle is from a *biblical* perspective.

~

THREE

What Is a Miracle?

The historian Edward Gibbon listed the miraculous powers ascribed to the early church as one of five reasons for the phenomenal growth of Christianity in the Roman Empire.[1] Miracles were and *still are* very important to Christianity. Indeed, Christianity is a religion of miracles. *But just what is a miracle?*

Today the term is used so loosely that it has practically been robbed of its historical meaning. An NFL quarterback makes a fabulous pass from the fifty-yard line that leads to a touchdown in the last three seconds of the game, and we call it a miracle. Someone drives to the mall the week before Christmas, and there is a parking place right by the entrance— a miracle! A student comes home and says, "It was a miracle I passed that final exam." A woman arrives at a luncheon and tells her friends, "It was a miracle I made it here on time." We shop for detergents to make our clothes "miracle white." We watch a children's movie on television called *Miracle on Thirty-Fourth Street,* in which the word "miracle" essentially relates to the world of myth.

In view of this loose use of the term, Bible scholar Robert Dean understandably urges "we must be careful not to use the word so generally that the result makes so many things miraculous that the word loses its meaning. This kind of 'inflation of miracles' dilutes God's divine standard, so that a phenomenon which really belongs in the realm of the ordinary is wrongly labeled as a miracle."[2] Dean is right. We must be careful in how we define miracles lest they lose all significance to us.

Inadequate Definitions of Miracles

In addressing the definition of miracles, it is helpful to begin by briefly making note of the two most common *inadequate* definitions that have surfaced from time to time throughout church history. The first inadequate definition of a miracle is this: "God working in the world *without using means* to bring about the results He wishes."[3] This definition is inadequate because many of the miracles recorded in the Bible did in fact use "means." For example, when Jesus fed 5000 people, He multiplied two fishes and five loaves of bread into enough food to feed the crowd. (The fish and bread were "means.") When Jesus turned water into wine at the wedding feast, He obviously used the "means" of water.[4] So this definition does not suffice.

A second inadequate definition is this: "An event impossible to explain by natural causes."[5] At first glance this definition might seem to be a good one. But the definition fails because it gives no recognition to God as being the author of the miracle. In this definition, miracles can just "happen" with no involvement of the divine necessary. This type of definition seems to be the one adopted by some of today's television shows on miracles.

Bible scholar Richard Purtill is right when he says that a miracle "must be caused *by the power of God*. If for some reason we find that some apparently wonderful event can be accounted for by some power less than the power of God, then we withhold the designation 'miracle.'"[6] In what follows, Purtill's point will be substantiated.

Properly Defining Miracles

The English word "miracle" comes from the Latin term *miraculum,* which merely refers to something that evokes wonder.[7] Theologians have wrestled long and hard to find the best way to define the term from a biblical perspective.

- Herbert Lockyer, for example, defines a miracle as "a work wrought by a divine power for a divine purpose by means beyond the reach of man."[8]

- C. S. Lewis defines a miracle as "an interference with nature by supernatural power."[9]

- J. Gresham Machen defines a miracle as "an event in the external world that is wrought by the immediate power of God."[10]

- J. I. Packer says a miracle is "an observed event that triggers awareness of God's presence and power."[11]

- Merrill F. Unger says miracles may be defined as "supernatural manifestations of divine power in the external world, in themselves special revelations of the presence and power of God; and in connection with other special revelations to which they are subservient, as aiding in their attestation, establishment, and preservation."[12]

- The *Wycliffe Bible Encyclopedia* tells us that "a miracle occurs when God steps in to do something beyond what could be accomplished according to the laws of nature as we understand them....Moreover, a miracle is beyond man's intellectual or scientific ability."[13]

Apologist Norman L. Geisler is correct in pointing out that in a broad sense, every supernaturally caused event described in Scripture is miraculous. But he notes that Scripture also uses the concept in a narrower, more technical sense.[14] It is this narrower sense that I want to focus on at the outset of this chapter. Then I will address the "looser," nontechnical sense of the word.

Actually, Scripture has no single word that is translated "miracle." In view of this, I think the best way to come to an accurate understanding of what constitutes a "miracle" is to examine each of the four primary Greek words Scripture uses for "miracle" and then compile what we learn into a single definition. That way, we understand what the Bible itself means by "miracle"—as opposed to the loose way the term is often used today.

New Testament Terms for "Miracle"

The four Greek words we will focus attention on are typically translated "miracle" or "mighty work" *(dunamis)*, "sign" *(semeion)*, "wonder" *(terata)*, and "work" *(erga)*. These terms are often used together with each other in referring to the miraculous acts of God.

Mighty Works—Dunamis

The Greek word *dunamis* literally means "strength," "power," "ability," "inherent power," "power residing in a thing by virtue of its nature," "power for performing miracles."[15] *Vine's Expository Dictionary of Biblical Words* tells us that the word is used "of works of a supernatural origin and character, such as could not be produced by natural agents and means."[16] Whoever the human instrument might be in the accomplishment (such as an apostle), the mighty power itself is *of God alone.*[17] In the New Testament, the word can be translated "miracles" or "mighty works."

In Acts 8:13, for example, we read, "Simon himself believed and was baptized. And he followed Philip everywhere, astonished by the great signs and *miracles* he saw" (emphasis added). In Acts 19:11 we read "God did extraordinary *miracles* through Paul" (emphasis added). Jesus once said, "Woe to you, Korazin! Woe to you, Bethsaida! If the *miracles* that were performed in you had been performed in Tyre and Sidon, they would have repented long ago in sackcloth and ashes" (Matthew 11:21, emphasis added). In each case, these miracles involved mighty works of God.

Sign—Semeion

The Greek word *semeion* literally means "sign," "mark," "token," "that by which a person or a thing is distinguished from others and is known."[18] *Vine's Expository Dictionary of Biblical Words* tells us that the word is often used of miracles and wonders as *signs of divine authority.*[19]

Richard Mayhue, vice president and dean of The Master's Seminary, tells us that *semeion* "leads a person to something beyond the miracle. It is valuable not for what it is, but rather for what it points toward."[20] Baptist preacher Adrian Rogers tells us that *semeion* carries the idea of "miracle with the message" or a "miracle with a meaning." It is a "miracle with a special lesson tied to it."[21] Josh McDowell and Don Stewart say the word conveys the idea of an "attesting miracle or a miraculous proof."[22] Greek scholar Spiros Zodhiates tells us that *semeion* refers to a "sign, mark, token, miracle with a spiritual end and purpose...which lead to something out of and beyond themselves; fingermarks of God, valuable not so much for what they are as for what they indicate of the grace and power of the Doer."[23] In the New Testament the word is most often translated "signs."

For example, regarding Jesus' miracle of turning water into wine, we read: "This, the first of his *miraculous signs,* Jesus performed at Cana in Galilee. He thus revealed his glory, and his disciples put their faith in him" (John 2:11, emphasis added). Similarly, after Jesus healed a royal official's son, we read that "this was the second *miraculous sign* that Jesus performed, having come from Judea to Galilee" (John 4:54, emphasis added). John 6:2 tells us that a great crowd of people followed Jesus because "they saw the *miraculous signs* he had performed on the sick" (emphasis added). After Jesus raised His friend Lazarus from the dead, we read that "many people, because they had heard that he had given this *miraculous sign,* went out to meet him" (John 12:18, emphasis added).

In contexts dealing with Jesus, it is evident that the "signs" are to be considered as objective pointers to His identity as the promised divine Messiah. As Isaiah 35 makes clear, one of the credentials of the divine Messiah would be that He would perform signs and miracles (such as giving sight to the blind and enabling the lame to walk) among the people. Jesus fulfilled these Old Testament prophecies perfectly. The apostle John selected seven miracles of Jesus to write about in his Gospel, and in each case he called them "signs." The most magnificent miracle of the New Testament—the resurrection of Jesus from the dead—is also called a *sign* (the "sign of Jonah") in Matthew 12:39.

In contexts dealing with the apostles, the *signs* attested that these individuals were genuine messengers of God (see Hebrews 2:3,4).[24] The signs or miracles conveyed to witnesses the stamp of the presence and power of God in the apostle. Merrill F. Unger says these signs "reveal the connection of the one who works them with the spiritual world and are thus seals attending his authority as a messenger from God

(John 2:18,23; 3:2; Matthew 12:38; Acts 14:3; 2 Corinthians 12:12)."[25] *Where miracles are, there certainly God is.* The man who works a miracle thereby affords clear proof that he comes with the authority of God; they are his credentials that he is God's messenger.[26] Recall that when Paul was defending his authority as an apostle of God, he reminded the Corinthian believers that "the things that mark an apostle—*signs, wonders and miracles*—were done among you with great perseverance" (2 Corinthians 12:12, emphasis added).

In the Old Testament, the prophet Moses is said to have performed "signs." The first appearance of the term comes in God's prediction given to Moses that Israel would be delivered from Egypt to serve God at Mount Horeb. God said, "I will be with you. And this will be the *sign* to you that it is I who have sent you: When you have brought the people out of Egypt, you will worship God on this mountain" (Exodus 3:12, emphasis added). In accomplishing the task assigned to him by God, Moses performed various signs (such as turning a rod into a serpent and making his hand turn leprous) to demonstrate that he was truly sent from God (4:1-7). When Moses performed these signs, the people believed (4:30,31). Moses later challenged Israel with the words: "Has any god ever tried to take for himself one nation out of another nation, by testings, by *miraculous signs* and wonders, by war, by a mighty hand and an outstretched arm, or by great and awesome deeds, like all the things the LORD your God did for you in Egypt before your very eyes?" (Deuteronomy 4:34, emphasis added). Moses also reminded the people, "Before our eyes the LORD sent *miraculous signs* and wonders—great and terrible—upon Egypt and Pharaoh and his whole household" (Deuteronomy 6:22, emphasis added).

To recap then, "signs" are miracles that point beyond themselves. In contexts dealing with Jesus, they attest to His identity as the divine Messiah. In contexts dealing with prophets and apostles, they serve to validate them as spokesmen for God.

Wonder—Terata

The Greek word *terata* literally means "wonder." It refers to something that evokes astonishment or amazement in the beholder.[27] Such miracles "make us catch our breath or drop our jaws."[28] They "produce astonishment as being outside the ordinary operations of cause and effect."[29]

In its 16 New Testament usages, the word *wonder* is used side by side with the word *sign*.[30] For example, Peter, preaching about the crucified and resurrected Christ, said: "Men of Israel, listen to this: Jesus of Nazareth was a man accredited by God to you by miracles, *wonders and signs,* which God did among you through him, as you yourselves know" (Acts 2:22, emphasis added). Moreover, the message of salvation preached by the apostles was attested "by *signs, wonders* and various miracles" (Hebrews 2:4, emphasis added). It makes sense that these words are often found side by side in Scripture. After all, the miracles in question are often so incredible that they 1) cause astonishment *(wonder),* and 2) cause one to recognize that the person performing the astonishing miracle *must* be a spokesman for God *(sign).*

Works—Erga

The Greek word *erga* literally means "works." The word is used by Jesus to describe His distinctive works—those works that no one else has done. For example, we read "when John had heard in the prison *the works* of Christ, he sent two of his disciples, and said unto him, Art thou he that should come, or do we look for another?" (Matthew 11:2,3 KJV, emphasis added). Jesus spoke of His miraculous works in an effort to spur people to believe in Him: "Though ye believe not me, believe *the works*: that ye may know, and believe, that the Father is in me, and I in him" (John 10:38 KJV, emphasis added). These are works that no mere human can do. These works point to divine power.

Compiling the Four Greek Words

On the basis of the four Greek words we've discussed, we might concisely define a miracle as a unique and extraordinary event awakening wonder *(terata),* wrought by divine power *(dunamis),* accomplishing some practical and benevolent work *(erga),* and authenticating or signifying a messenger and his message as from God *(semeion).* As noted previously, a number of Bible verses use two or three of these terms at the same time to refer to a miracle of God (see Acts 2:22; 4:30; 5:12; Hebrews 2:4; 2 Corinthians 12:12).

According to this very narrow definition, many of the things that are called "miracles" in our day fail to measure up to the biblical standard. Yet that doesn't mean that God is not doing supernatural things in our midst today. *He is!* Let us continue to clarify the teaching of Scripture on this matter so that we may attain a complete perspective.

Miracles of Providence— Grade B Miracles

How does one define an act of God today that is obviously supernatural but does not necessarily fit the very narrow definition given above? Scholars disagree on how to answer this question. Many scholars prefer to use the term "providential act" instead of "miracle" to describe how God often acts today. Others prefer to say that there is both a *strict* definition and a *looser* definition of "miracle." The strict definition focuses on the *sign* miracles of New Testament times (such as turning water into wine, walking on water, and raising someone from the dead). The looser definition can be used in relation to some of God's providential acts in our lives (such as when the milk truck broke down in front of George Müller's orphanage, thereby providing much-needed milk for the breakfasts of the hungry orphans).

It is important to understand that the lesser *providential* miracle involves the hand of God every bit as much as the greater *sign* miracle. Both are rooted in the divine. As Reformed scholar Charles Hodge put it, "The importance of what are called providential miracles is not lessened by their being thrown into a class by themselves. They continue to be clear evidence of divine intervention."[31]

Personally, I like Henry Morris's designation of the *sign* miracles as "Grade A miracles" and the *providential* miracles as "Grade B miracles." Morris writes:

> Two kinds of miracles are possible: Those which intervene in the operation of natural processes, and those which contravene basic law. For purposes of discussion, we may call these, respectively, miracles of providence and miracles of creation, or, if informality is permitted, Grade B miracles and Grade A miracles.[32]

To illustrate, the various sign miracles of Jesus recorded in the Gospel of John are clearly Grade A miracles:

> The simple molecular structure of water was instantly raised to the more complex structure of wine; the nobleman's son, beyond all hope of life, was suddenly and completely revived; the incurably atrophied cripple at the pool of Bethesda was instantly given full soundness of physique; a great amount of bread and meat was created to feed the five thousand; a new kind of antigravitational energy was created to enable Jesus to walk on the sea; a man born without eyesight suddenly had perfect eyes; and Lazarus, decaying in

the grave, was restored to life. All of these miracles demanded God's creative power, and they were climaxed by the resurrection of Christ Himself, by His own power (see John 10:18).[33]

Grade B miracles, by contrast, are providentially accomplished within the framework of nature's basic laws—but nevertheless involve God's activity. One example might be the event described in Acts 16 in which a mighty earthquake occurred and caused Paul and Silas's chains to break loose and the prison doors to open (see verse 26). A rank unbeliever might say this was just a freak coincidence. But the context indicates that it was an act of God. The timing and circumstances of the earthquake point to divine activity.[34] As R. C. Trench put it, "the finger of God may be so plainly discernible in [such an event] that even while it is plainly explicable by natural causes, we yet may be entirely justified in terming it a miracle, a providential, although not an absolute, miracle."[35]

Bible scholar Winfried Corduan provides this excellent example of how the circumstances and timing of an event can point to the miraculous:

> Sometimes an event can be explained in terms of natural laws, and yet believers may claim that it was a miracle. In many such cases, it is the coming together of certain natural events—their "constellation"—that makes the event unusual. Let us say that a believer—call him Bill Smith—loses his application for employment on the way to mailing it. A strong wind carries it across town, where it gets stuck between the cab and bed of a produce truck that happens to be going to the very city where Bill's prospective employer is headquartered. As the truck is parked at its destination overnight, vandals ransack the truck and so dislodge the letter. The letter lies on the sidewalk until the next morning, when it is picked up by a jogger, the

daughter of the company president. She presents it to her father, who reads the application and hires Bill.

Meanwhile, Bill has been asking God to intervene on his behalf since he lost the application. When Bill gets a phone call from the president of the company, he thanks God for a miracle. As a believer in God, he is justified in this assessment, though it would admittedly not satisfy a naturalist. Bill recognizes that the event is highly unusual; the fact that he prayed clinches it for him that God intervened, and so he feels justified in identifying the event as miraculous....

Norman Geisler refers to it as a "class 2" miracle.* The aspect of the situation that calls special attention to divine agency is...the coming together of the number of events that are in themselves physically possible...to form a constellation of events that is highly improbable.[36]

I believe that today God often performs such "Grade B" (or "second class") miracles. For example, I believe a Grade B miracle occurred when my pastor sent a postcard to Sally (who found out she was having a Down's Syndrome baby), and it was misdelivered to the address of another Christian lady (miles away) who *already had* a Down's Syndrome child, and who subsequently ended up helping Sally. This was not any kind of *sign* miracle such as we see recorded in the Gospel of John. But God's supernatural providential work is clearly evident in this situation.

---

* Geisler writes: "It may be that some things are so highly unusual and coincidental that, when viewed in connection with the moral or theological context in which they occurred, the label 'miracle' is the most appropriate one for the happening. Let us call this kind of supernaturally guided event a second-class miracle, that is, one whose natural process can be described scientifically (and perhaps even replicated by humanly controlled natural means) but whose end product in the total picture is best explained by invoking the supernatural." (Norman L. Geisler, *Christian Apologetics* [Grand Rapids, Michigan: Baker Book House, 1976], p. 277.)

Healing and Providential Miracles

One way we might illustrate Grade B miracles relates to healing. Most of us as Christians can point to personal experiences we've had in which God answered prayer regarding the need for someone's physical healing. In many of these cases, the healing involved visits to a doctor or even a stay in the hospital. In such a medical setting, God works providentially over time to bring about the desired healing.

Now, God *could* bring about an instant healing (a Grade A miracle). But often God, in His infinite wisdom, decides to perform a Grade B (providential) miracle instead. Pastor Douglas Connelly wisely tells us: "In both situations God is actively at work. God is just as much involved in a gradual, providential recovery as He is in an instantaneous, miraculous healing. God simply chooses to work in different ways depending on His desired purpose."[37]

There are also times when God chooses *not to heal at all.* The apostle Paul himself experienced such a situation (see 2 Corinthians 12:7-10). It is important for us to recognize that God has not promised to deliver us *from* every painful situation, but He has promised to walk with us *through* every such situation. Sometimes God has a purpose in allowing us to go through times of suffering (see 1 Peter 4:15-19; also chapter 14 of this book, "If Your Miracle Doesn't Come," deals with the issue).

Angels and Providential Miracles

Scripture is clear that on occasion God may choose to utilize His holy angels in bringing about a Grade B providential miracle. Certainly God does not have to depend upon angels in order to bring about such miracles. In fact, He is most often portrayed as bringing about miracles without angelic involvement. Nevertheless, it is *sometimes* God's sovereign will to use angels to bring about such miracles.

One example of this is found in the book of Revelation, where God is portrayed as pouring down His judgments on an unbelieving world. In Revelation 8:7-13, for example, we read that hail and fire will fall upon the earth, and a third of the grass and trees will be burned up. We read that something like a huge blazing mountain (an asteroid?) will crash into the sea and kill a third of the living creatures in the sea and destroy a third of the ships. Behind all of these future events is angelic activity. These events *seem* to be natural disasters, but behind these natural disasters is the work of angels assigned by God. Henry Morris tells us that the book of Revelation "especially describes angels as capable, under God, of unleashing terrific natural phenomena—hail, fire, meteorites, or other heavenly bodies, even of controlling the rate of nuclear processes of the sun (Revelation 8:7-12; 16:8), as well as physical plagues on human flesh (Revelation 16:2,10)."[38] (For more on angels, see my book *Angels Among Us: Separating Fact from Fiction,* published by Harvest House Publishers.)

The Purpose of Miracles

Now that we understand what miracles are from a biblical perspective, let us proceed to briefly examine what Scripture says about the *purpose* of miracles. I've already touched on some of this in passing, but the following presents the complete picture.

Miracles Accredit God's Messengers

As noted previously, God's miracles in biblical times often served to confirm certain messengers as being God's representatives. This includes the prophets, the apostles, and especially Jesus Christ Himself.[39] For example, in Acts 2:22 we read Peter's words to the Jews: "Men of Israel, listen to this: Jesus of Nazareth was a man *accredited by God to you by miracles, wonders and signs,* which God did among you through him, as you yourselves know" (emphasis added). Nicodemus said to Jesus: "We know you are a teacher who has come from God. For no one could perform the miraculous *signs* you are doing if God were not with him" (John 3:2, emphasis added).

Miracles Confirm God's Message

Besides confirming God's *messengers,* Scripture tells us that miracles often serve to confirm God's *message.* In Hebrews 2:3,4 we read: "How shall we escape if we ignore such a great salvation? This salvation, which was first announced by the Lord, *was confirmed to us* by those who heard him. God also *testified to it by signs, wonders and various miracles,* and gifts of the Holy Spirit distributed according to his will" (emphasis added).

In Acts 14:3 we likewise read that Paul and Barnabas's message of grace was confirmed by miracles: "So Paul and Barnabas spent considerable time there [in Iconium], speaking boldly for the Lord, who *confirmed the message of his grace by enabling them to do miraculous signs and wonders*" (emphasis added, insert added).

Miracles Bring Glory to God and Jesus

Another purpose of miracles, according to Scripture, is to bring glory to God and Jesus. After Jesus performed the miracle of turning water into wine, for example, we read: "This, the first of his miraculous signs, Jesus performed at Cana in Galilee. He thus revealed his glory, and his disciples put their faith in him" (John 2:11). After Jesus healed a paralytic, the crowds "were awestruck, and glorified God" (Matthew 9:8 NASB). The people glorified God when they saw Jesus heal the paralytic lowered through the roof (Luke 5:24-26), when Jesus raised the widow of Nain's son from the dead (Luke 7:16), when He healed a woman bent over double by a spirit (Luke 13:13,17), and when He healed the blind man (Luke 18:42,43).

In the Old Testament, Moses' miracles in the Exodus account manifest God's great glory. Consider God's own words to Moses:

> Raise your staff and stretch out your hand over the sea to divide the water so that the Israelites can go through the sea on dry ground. I will harden the hearts of the Egyptians so that they will go in after them. And *I will gain glory* through Pharaoh and all his army, through his chariots and his horsemen. The Egyptians will know that I am the LORD *when I gain glory* through Pharaoh, his chariots and his horsemen (Exodus 14:16-18, emphasis added).

Miracles Demonstrate the Presence of God's Kingdom

Yet another purpose of miracles is to show that God's kingdom has come and is expanding as it brings beneficial results into peoples' lives. Jesus said, "If it is by the Spirit of God that I cast out demons, then the kingdom of God has come upon you" (Matthew 12:28 RSV). Likewise, Jesus gave His disciples "power and authority over all demons and to cure diseases, and he sent them out to preach the kingdom of God and to heal" (Luke 9:1,2 RSV).

Miracles Promote Faith

An important practical purpose of miracles is to engender faith among God's people.[40] We read in Exodus 14:31, "When the Israelites saw the great power the LORD displayed against the Egyptians, the people feared the LORD and put their trust in him and in Moses his servant." John 20:30,31 tells us, "Jesus did many other miraculous signs in the presence of his disciples, which are not recorded in this book. But these are written that you may believe that Jesus is the Christ, the Son of God, and that by believing you may have life in his name."

Miracles Demonstrate God's Sovereignty

Yet another purpose of miracles, according to Scripture, is to demonstrate the sovereignty of God. We read God's own words in Exodus 7:5: "The Egyptians will know that I am the LORD when I stretch out my hand against Egypt and bring the Israelites out of it." Then, during the wilderness sojourn, God's miraculous provisions continued to show God's sovereignty: "During the forty years that I led you through the desert, your clothes did not wear out, nor did the sandals on your feet....I did this so that you might know that I am the LORD your God" (Deuteronomy 29:5,6). God's miracles demonstrate His control over the affairs of humans.

Miracles Help People in Need

A final and very important purpose of miracles is to help people in need. The two blind men near Jericho cried out, "Have mercy on us," and Jesus "in pity" healed them (Matthew 20:30,34). When Jesus beheld a great crowd of people, "he had compassion on them and healed their sick" (Matthew 14:14).[41] All throughout the New Testament, we witness the miracles of Jesus helping people in need.

In the next chapter, I will examine in detail a prime example of God using miracles to help people in need. Indeed, God used His mighty miracles to deliver the enslaved Israelites from harsh Egyptian bondage.

~

FOUR

Miracles in
the Old Testament

The Old Testament lays an important foundation for our study of miracles, for in it we read how God often makes Himself known by miraculous signs and wonders. Indeed, God is often portrayed as distinguishing Himself from the false gods of pagan nations by the mighty works He performs.

While there are many miracles worthy of our attention in the Old Testament, I intend to limit my focus in the present chapter to the signs and wonders related to God's deliverance of the Israelites from Egypt. The miraculous element in this deliverance is spoken of often in Scripture:

- In Exodus 7:3 God affirmed His intention to "multiply my *miraculous signs and wonders* in Egypt" (emphasis added).

- In Deuteronomy 6:22 Moses said, "Before our eyes the LORD sent *miraculous signs and wonders*—great and terrible—upon Egypt and Pharaoh and his whole household" (emphasis added).

- In Deuteronomy 7:19 Moses told the people, "You saw with your own eyes the great trials, the *miraculous signs and wonders,* the mighty hand and outstretched arm, with which the LORD your God brought you out" (emphasis added).

- In Deuteronomy 26:8 Moses again said, "So the LORD brought us out of Egypt with a mighty hand and an outstretched arm, with great terror and with *miraculous signs and wonders*" (emphasis added).

- In Nehemiah 9:10 the prophet recalls to God, "You sent *miraculous signs and wonders* against Pharaoh, against all his officials and all the people of his land, for you knew how arrogantly the Egyptians treated them. You made a name for yourself, which remains to this day" (emphasis added).

- In Psalm 135:9 we read that God "sent his *signs and wonders* into your midst, O Egypt, against Pharaoh and all his servants" (emphasis added).

- In Jeremiah 32:20 the prophet affirms to God, "You performed *miraculous signs and wonders* in Egypt and have continued them to this day, both in Israel and among all mankind, and have gained the renown that is still yours" (emphasis added).

Clearly, if there is any series of miracles of great renown in Old Testament times, it is those signs and wonders that God performed while delivering the Israelites from Egyptian bondage. *Any* ancient Jew would tell you the same.

I begin with the recognition that Moses once said to God, "Who among the gods is like you, O LORD? Who is like you—majestic in holiness, awesome in glory, working wonders?" (Exodus 15:11). What gave birth to such lofty thinking in the mind of Moses? What happened in the ancient past that caused him to so exalt God's name? Especially in view of the polytheism he was exposed to as a child in Egypt,* why did

---

*Polytheism is the belief in many gods.

Moses given his sole allegiance to the God of the Bible above all the other gods? The answer is simple. Moses had a "close encounter" with the one true God. He experienced the *incomparable* One who has no rival!

A key emphasis throughout the first five books of the Bible is that the one true God of the Bible, whose name is Yahweh, is *incomparable.* Moses expressed this incomparability in two different ways, the most common being by *negation.* The negation was usually couched in words such as "There is no one like the LORD our God" (Exodus 8:10). Having been exposed to all the gods of Egypt during his childhood, Moses was no doubt qualified to make such judgments, especially after experiencing Yahweh's superlative power as miraculously manifested in the Exodus account.

A second way Moses expressed the incomparability of Yahweh was by using rhetorical questions. He often asked, "Who among the gods is like you, O LORD?" (Exodus 15:11). Of course, the implied answer is "no one in all the universe."

Even to the present day, scholars are unsure about the total number of gods the Egyptians worshiped. Most lists contain somewhere in the neighborhood of 80 deities.[1] The dedication of the Egyptians to their gods is evident even to the casual observer as he tours modern Egypt. Beautiful temples honoring various gods virtually fill the landscape. The ancient Egyptians truly paid homage to the many gods they worshiped.

In Egyptian religion, the god at the top of the totem pole was the sun god, *Re.* Next in line was the Pharaoh of Egypt, who was considered to be the son of *Re.*[2] Hence, the Pharaoh of Egypt was himself considered a god in his own right. Inasmuch as Re was deemed superior to all other gods, his son—the Pharaoh—was also considered to possess unmatched power as a god. This adds a whole new dimension to the Exodus account. It is as if a *contest* occurs between the true

God on the one side and Pharaoh and the false gods of Egypt on the other side (see Numbers 33:4).

As the Exodus account makes clear, Pharaoh reacted to the various displays of Yahweh's incomparability (as manifested in the ten miraculous plagues) by hardening his heart against Yahweh. He was no doubt stunned in disbelief that a "foreign God" could come into his territory, make shambles of all the gods of his land, and make him *(the mighty son of Re)* appear impotent before his own people. Furthermore, the representatives of this "foreign God" (Moses and Aaron) were both in the neighborhood of 80 years old when they encountered young Pharaoh.[3] How dare the youthful Pharaoh's power and authority be challenged in such a humiliating way by two old guys!

It all started this way one fateful day: Moses and Aaron appeared before the Pharaoh of Egypt and said: "This is what the LORD, the God of Israel, says: 'Let my people go, so that they may hold a festival to me in the desert'" (Exodus 5:1). This meeting may have taken place at one of the temples associated with some aspect of the Nile's sacredness.[4] Pharaoh may even have been worshiping or performing a sacred rite in one of these temples when Moses and Aaron approached.

Pharaoh responded by asking the question of the century: "Who is the LORD [Yahweh] that I should obey him and let Israel go?" (Exodus 5:2). The Pharaoh was aware that he himself was the son of Re, and was hence considered to be a great god.[5] He also knew there were literally scores of gods who were worshiped in varying degrees by his people. But *who was Yahweh* that Pharaoh should obey him? Pharaoh's question would soon be answered.

In what follows, I want you to keep in mind God's oft-repeated twofold purpose in inflicting these ten miraculous plagues upon the Egyptians. *To the Jews:* "You will know that I am the LORD your God, who brought you out from under the yoke of the Egyptians" (Exodus 6:7). *To the Egyptians:* You "will know that I am the Lord" (7:17); "...so that you will know that I, the Lord, am in this land" (8:22); "...so you may know that there is no one like me in all the earth" (9:14); "...so you may know that the earth is the Lord's" (9:29); "...that you may know that I am the Lord" (14:4); "...the Egyptians will know that I am the Lord" (14:18). *Obviously, the true God did not want to be misunderstood as to His purpose!* He wanted it to be utterly clear that there is one and *only* one true God in the universe.

The First Plague

Because Pharaoh had refused to let the Israelites go, Moses informed Pharaoh that the water of the Nile would be turned into blood (Exodus 7:17). As well, the streams, canals, ponds, and reservoirs that were connected to the Nile would be turned to blood (verse 19).

Some liberal commentators have feebly suggested that the river was not turned into literal blood, but was made to have the appearance of blood either by red clay that washed into the river or by reddish fungi in the river. However, this view fails to explain the *immediateness* of the river turning to blood when Aaron stretched out his staff over the water. Nor does it explain the extensive death of the fish of the Nile. To the Egyptians, the river had the actual appearance of blood—in terms of its taste, smell, *and* texture.

Without question, this miraculous plague would have jolted every Egyptian in the land. This was because they venerated the Nile and all that was associated with it. The river Nile was worshiped by the Egyptians under various names and symbols. It was considered the father of life, and in view of the fact that its water was the lifeblood of Egypt, the blow must have been devastating.[6] So revered was the Nile by the Egyptians that hymns were written in its honor. One such hymn begins, "Hail thee, O Nile, that issues from the earth and comes to keep Egypt alive!"[7]

This judgment presented the beginning of Moses' demonstration of the true God's miraculous power over the many false gods of Egypt.[8] Besides being a judgment against Pharaoh (the god-king), this plague also constituted a judgment against the Egyptian sacred river god, *Nilus*.[9] Since *Nilus* was worshiped by every Egyptian, this plague struck at the very heart of Egyptian religion.

Other false gods affected included *Khnum*, the alleged guardian of the Nile sources, and *Hapi*, the alleged spirit of the Nile. Furthermore, *Osiris* was believed to be a great god of the underworld whose bloodstream was the Nile river.[10] How ironic that God turned the Nile into *real* blood.

Not only did the fish in the river die, but "the river smelled so bad that the Egyptians could not drink its water" (Exodus 7:21). What a contrast this was to the Egyptian "Hymn to the Nile," which triumphantly proclaimed that the Nile River was "sweet of fragrance."

Still other false gods that would have been affected in lesser degrees include *Neith* (a god who watched over the larger fish of the Nile), and *Hathor* (protector of the smaller fish of the Nile).[11] To say the least, this plague convincingly demonstrated the total impotence of the gods of Egypt in the face of the incomparable and miraculous Yahweh.

Apparently the Egyptian sorcerers, by trickery and occultic enchantments, were able to turn small quantities of water into what appeared to be blood (though it would have been more beneficial if they had been able to turn the blood back into water—see Exodus 7:22). The water they turned to blood was likely small quantities taken from water holes dug in the ground (see verse 24), since the water of the Nile had already been completely turned into blood. Pharaoh seemed satisfied with his magician's apparent duplication, and his heart continued to harden against Moses and Aaron.

The Second Plague

The second miraculous plague resulted in a massive swarm of frogs (Exodus 8:1-15). This plague is particularly significant in view of the Egyptian veneration of frogs. The sacredness of the frog to the Egyptians is evident in the many amulets discovered that are shaped like frogs. Old Testament scholar John Davis observes: "The common presence of the frog to the Egyptians was not something loathsome or to be abhorred. The frogs, to a large degree, represented fruitfulness, blessing, and the assurance of the harvest."[12]

So honored were frogs by the Egyptians that they were deified, and the Egyptians made a representation of the goddess *Heqt* in the image of a frog. Heqt was considered an emblem of fertility, and it was believed she assisted Egyptian women in the bearing of children.[13]

The Egyptian veneration of frogs is also evident in the fact that the intentional killing of a frog was punishable by death.[14] Hence, when this plague was inflicted on the Egyptians, it must have been abominable to them in that everywhere they stepped, they crushed a frog.

Not willing to be outdone, Pharaoh's magicians were called in to demonstrate that the gods of Egypt were equal to Yahweh. The magicians were able to bring up some frogs upon the land (Exodus 8:7), but they proved incapable of *removing* the plague. Accordingly, Pharaoh requested Moses to "pray to the Lord" (Yahweh) that the plague would be removed. Pharaoh even promised that Israel would be permitted to leave Egypt and sacrifice to Yahweh.

To further demonstrate the incomparability of Yahweh, Moses asked Pharaoh to specifically name the time when he wanted the plague to end. Pharaoh asked Moses to have it removed the following day. Moses answered: "It will be as you say, so that you may know there is no one like the LORD [Yahweh] our God" (Exodus 8:10).

Why didn't Pharaoh ask for the plague to terminate immediately? More than likely, he hoped that the frogs would go away on their own, under which circumstances he would be under no obligation to Moses or Yahweh. Nevertheless, despite the fact that "there was relief" and the plague ended the following day, Pharaoh again hardened his heart and refused to honor the promise he had made to Moses. He could not bring himself to admit that Yahweh was indeed the incomparable One with no rival.

The Third Plague

The third miraculous plague resulted in a devastating swarm of gnats (Exodus 8:16-19). Such gnats were so small that they were nearly invisible to the human eye, but they delivered a very painful and irritating sting.[15] The bite of such an insect caused a sore to develop, and numerous bites would virtually cover a person's skin with small sores.

It is not clear what specific deities this plague was directed against (with the exception of the god-king, Pharaoh). It is possible, however, that this plague was intended to humiliate the official priesthood in Egypt. These priests were well-known for their physical purity and attention to bodily care. "They were circumcised, shaved the hair from their heads and bodies, washed frequently, and were dressed in beautiful linen robes."[16] The gnats would have likely made their existence especially miserable. Furthermore, their prayers would have been made ineffective by their own personal impurity resulting from the bites all over their bodies. This would have resulted in a paralysis of the entire Egyptian religious system.

Up to this point, the Egyptian magicians (perhaps by sleight of hand) had been duplicating the miracles of Moses. But this is not the case with the present plague and those that follow. As Bible scholar Alan Cole observes, "Here, for the first time, the sorcerers fail. At last they know that Moses and Aaron are not producing conjuring tricks, by sleight of hand, as presumably they themselves have been doing all along. They admit that this is God at work."[17] Upon the infliction of this plague, the Egyptians have begun to discover the incomparable nature of Yahweh. They discover that only the one true God can do *true* miracles.

The Fourth Plague

The fourth plague resulted in an overwhelming swarm of flies (Exodus 8:20-32). The bloodsucking "gadfly" or "dogfly" was abhorred in Egypt and may have been partially responsible for the prevalence of blindness in the land.[18]

That this plague was supernatural is clear from the fact that the land of Goshen (where the Israelites were staying) was untouched by the swarm of flies (Exodus 8:22). The plague was directed only against Egypt and its false gods.

Among the false gods this judgment was directed against was Beelzebub, the god of the flies.[19] This god was thought to have the power to prevent flies. But as had been true all along, Beelzebub, like the other gods, was nowhere to be found when this plague occurred.

Again, in view of the cleanliness which was necessary for proper Egyptian worship, the putrid conditions brought about by the unclean flies would have been a great hindrance to the idol priests of Egypt. The plague likely brought religious worship in Egypt to a total standstill.

In view of his complete inability to cope with the situation, Pharaoh called for Moses and Aaron and offered them a compromise. He said he would allow the Israelites to sacrifice to Yahweh, but only on the condition that they would do it within the boundaries of Egypt (Exodus 8:25). This, of course, was not acceptable to Moses. Pharaoh then offered a second compromise in which he said he would allow them to go into the wilderness, assuming that they would not go very far (verse 28). Moses went along with this, but warned Pharaoh not to continue dealing deceitfully with the people of God. He then promised Pharaoh that the plague would end the following day.

Once freed from the devastation of this plague, Pharaoh again hardened his heart against Yahweh and went back on his promise (Exodus 8:32). This god-king just couldn't find it in himself to submit to a foreign God, especially in view of the fact that all of Egypt was watching how their mighty leader was reacting to this outside invasion.

The Fifth Plague

The fifth plague resulted in many Egyptian animals becoming diseased (Exodus 9:1-7). To further substantiate the miraculous nature of this plague, the Lord announced a set time for the beginning of this disaster, and this time was precisely fulfilled as announced in Exodus 9:6. Furthermore, not a single one of the Israelite animals was afflicted.

The Egyptians believed every animal to be sacred because various gods were thought to inhabit their bodies. Legend has it that when the giants made war on the gods, the gods were all forced to flee to Egypt and take refuge in the bodies of various animals. Such animals were therefore sacred, protected, and worshiped. It was with this knowledge that, according to scholar Alan Cole, "the Persians unfairly won a battle against the Egyptians in the days of Cambyses by driving a 'screen' of sacred animals ahead of them, at which no Egyptian bowman would shoot."[20]

This belief led the Egyptians to create images of the gods in the form of animals. For example, the God *Jupiter* was adored in the form of a ram; *Apollo* in the form of a crow; *Bacchus* as a goat; *Juno* as a heifer; *Diana* as a cat; *Venus* as a fish; and so forth.[21]

Further support for the Egyptian veneration of animals is found in the necropolis of sacred bulls, which was discovered near Memphis (in Egypt), an area well-known for its worship of both *Ptah* and the sacred *Apis* bulls. The Apis bull was thought to be the sacred animal of the god Ptah; hence, the associated worship of the Apis bull at Memphis is readily understood. At any one time, there was only one sacred Apis bull. As soon as one died, another was chosen to take its place. Such sacred bulls were supposed to have been recognized by 28 distinctive marks that identified them as divine and indicated they were to become objects of worship.[22]

Among other gods affected by this plague are *Hathor* (a goddess of love, beauty, and joy represented in the form of a cow), and *Mnevis* (a sacred bull venerated at Heliopolis and often associated with the sun-god *Re*).[23] All these "gods" were powerless when this deadly disease was inflicted upon them by the hand of the incomparable and miraculous Yahweh.

In view of the fact that all animals were believed to be inhabited by a god, this plague struck at the very heart of Egypt's religious system. All of Egypt must have mourned that day. How much would it take for the Egyptians to learn that there is no one like Yahweh?

The Sixth Plague

The sixth miraculous plague resulted in both men and beasts breaking out with boils and sores (Exodus 9:8-12). This was a severe inflammation that caused the flesh to burn and swell.[24] The infections here described may have been similar to those that Job once suffered (Job 2:7).

The Egyptians were well aware of the ever-present possibility of infectious diseases and sores. This is reflected in their belief that *Sekhmet*, a lion-headed goddess, was considered to have the power of both creating epidemics and bringing them to an end. According to scholar John Davis, a special priesthood was devoted to *Sekhmet* called *Sunu*.[25]

Following this plague, the magicians were apparently called in again to attempt to vindicate the power of the gods of Egypt and to show that Yahweh's power was not unique. However, they were not only unable to duplicate this miracle but were apparently not even able to appear in the royal court because of the severity of this plague upon their own bodies (Exodus 9:11).

The Egyptians no doubt sought relief from their sores from many of the Egyptian deities charged with the responsibility of healing. Among these was *Imhotep*, who was considered the god of medicine and the guardian of healing sciences, and *Isis*, who was considered a goddess of healing.[26] Neither Pharaoh, the other false gods, nor the priests were able to undo what the incomparable and miraculous Yahweh did.

The Seventh Plague

The seventh miraculous plague was a very heavy hail that fell on the land (Exodus 9:13-35). This plague was preceded by a specific explanation to Pharaoh from God through Moses and Aaron: "This time I will send the full force of my plagues against you and against your officials and your people, so you may know that there is no one like me in all the earth" (verse 14). Furthermore, Yahweh said, "I have raised you up for this very purpose, that I might show you my power and that my name might be proclaimed in all the earth" (verse 16). There was to be no misunderstanding as to the significance of what was about to occur.

Moses and Aaron then issued a warning: "Give an order now to bring your livestock and everything you have in the field to a place of shelter, because the hail will fall on every man and animal that has not been brought in and is still out in the field, and they will die" (Exodus 9:19). This warning was heeded by many of Pharaoh's servants (verse 20), a fact that was no doubt distressing to the god-king of Egypt. How humiliating it must have been for him as he witnessed with his own eyes how his followers were obeying Moses and Aaron, representatives of an outside God.

As was true earlier, the supernatural element of this judgment is clear in view of the fact that there was no hail whatsoever in the land of Goshen (Exodus 9:26). This could not be explained away as a natural storm.

Among the gods this judgment was directed against are *Shu,* the Egyptian god of the atmosphere,[27] and *Osiris,* who sometimes functioned as a god of agriculture.[28] Also included would be *Nut,* the sky goddess whose task it was to ensure the blessings of the sun and warmth, and *Seth,* a deity responsible for watching after crops.[29] All of these gods were thought to have the power necessary to prevent such catastrophes from occurring. But they were impotent in the shadow of the incomparable Yahweh.

The violent rain and hail were so severe that Pharaoh had to call again on Moses and Aaron. This time Pharaoh the god-king made three concessions to them (Exodus 9:27): 1) he acknowledged he had sinned; 2) he acknowledged Yahweh was righteous (quite a concession, since he denied the existence of Yahweh in Exodus 5:2); and 3) he admitted that he and his people were wicked and had acted wrongly. His confession was probably undergirded with a high degree of insincerity, much like those of Saul (1 Samuel 15:24) and Nebuchadnezzar (Daniel 4:37).

In any event, relief from this plague did not change the heart of Pharaoh, and he continued to resist as he had on previous occasions (Exodus 9:34,35). His heart continued to harden against Yahweh. He still could not bring himself to admit his own power and authority were no match for that of the incomparable and miraculous Yahweh.

The Eighth Plague

The eighth miraculous plague resulted in a massive locust swarm (Exodus 10:1-20).[30] Such a swarm would have been devastating to Egypt. Individual locusts have the capability of eating their own weight daily. This type of locust swarm would have had a density of 100 to 200 million locusts per square mile, with the potential of destroying hundreds of square miles of land. Locusts such as these possess the ability to flap their wings nonstop for 17 hours and can cruise at an airspeed of up to 12 miles per hour. With an average density of 130 million locusts per square mile, the collective movement of the swarm would have ranged from a few miles to more than 60 miles in a single day.[31]

In addition to Pharaoh, this was also apparently a judgment against *Serapis,* the Egyptian god that was supposedly able to protect the land from locusts.[32] Yet Serapis was nowhere to be found on this somber day in Egypt. As was true with the earlier plagues, this one was inflicted by Yahweh "that you may know that I am the LORD"—and know, at the same time, that the false gods of Egypt are, in fact, *no gods at all* (see Exodus 10:2).

Pharaoh promptly called Moses and Aaron and offered them another compromise. He was willing to let the *men* in Israel worship, but not their wives or their children (Exodus 10:10,11). This was not acceptable to Moses and Aaron, and they were immediately driven out of Pharaoh's presence.

It did not take long for Pharaoh to realize, however, that he was confronted with a crisis of unparalleled proportions. He accordingly called Moses and Aaron back again "quickly" and offered another confession, even asking for forgiveness this time (Exodus 10:17). As with the earlier occasions, he probably did this more out of expediency than out of sincerity.

Moses subsequently prayed that the plague would end, "and the Lord changed the wind to a very strong west wind, which caught up the locusts and carried them into the Red Sea" (Exodus 10:19). Despite Yahweh's display of grace in ending the plague, Pharaoh's heart continued to harden and he would not let the Israelites go.

The Ninth Plague

The ninth plague resulted in darkness enveloping the land of Egypt for three days. The darkness was so thick that it could actually be felt (Exodus 10:21,22). Yet the Israelites had light where they lived—clearly indicating the selective nature of God's judgment.

This judgment was unquestionably against the Egyptian sun god, *Re*. Bible scholar C. J. Labuschagne alerts us to the fact that "the sun-god was not only regarded as the creator, father, and king of the gods, but his singular and exceptional character as creator and sustainer of all living things caused him to be looked upon as the most excellent, most distinguished god in the pantheon, and to be praised as the god who was stronger, mightier, and more divine than the other gods."[33] Scholar John Davis adds that "his faithfulness in providing the warmth and light of sun day after day without fail caused them to express great joy over the faithfulness of this deity."[34] The "Universalist Hymn to the Sun" proclaims: "Hail to thee, beautiful Re of every day, who rises at dawn without ceasing."[35] Hence, this judgment of darkness in the land would have dealt a blow to the strongest god in Egypt. Imagine how Pharaoh must have felt when he witnessed the impotence of the god who was considered to be his own father.

Of course, Re was not the only god affected by this plague. Other gods affected included *Aten* (the deified sun disc), *Atum* (the god of the setting sun), *Khepre* (who was another form of the sun god Re), *Hathor* and *Nut* (sky goddesses), and *Thoth* (a moon god of Hermopolis).[36]

In desperation, the Pharaoh again called on Moses and Aaron and offered a compromise. He offered to let the children of Israel go and worship God in the desert, but with the stipulation that their flocks and herds be left behind (Exodus 10:24). This was unacceptable to Moses and Aaron. After all, the Israelites needed the animals to offer sacrifices to God (verses 25,26).

Throughout this encounter, Pharaoh's heart continued to harden, and the Egyptian leader refused to let the Israelites go. Allowing the Israelites to go with no assurance they would return was just too much for Pharaoh. He became enraged and demanded that Moses once for all leave the royal court, saying: "The day you see my face you will die" (Exodus 10:28). Moses responded, "Just as you say. I will never appear before you again" (verse 29).

Of course, Moses and Aaron *did* appear before Pharaoh again in Exodus 12:31 at Pharaoh's summoning. In this latter encounter, Pharaoh ordered Moses and the Israelites to leave Egypt. We may thus understand Moses' words in Exodus 10:29 to refer to the fact that Moses and Aaron would not be *initiating* any more appearances before Pharaoh to bring messages from God.

The Tenth Plague

The tenth and final plague resulted in the death of the firstborn of all the land (Exodus 11:1–12:36). God issued a somber pronouncement to the Egyptians: "I will pass through Egypt and strike down every firstborn—both men and animals—and I will bring judgment on all the gods of Egypt. I am the Lord" (12:12).

This judgment was particularly devastating to Pharaoh because his firstborn would have eventually come to sit on his father's throne.[37] Furthermore, Pharaoh's son—by an act of the gods—was considered to have divine properties just like his father.[38] From the Egyptian point of view, it is hard to conceive of any stronger demonstration of the incomparability of Yahweh. Through this plague, "*all* the gods of Egypt" were judged (Exodus 12:12, emphasis added).

Among the gods who were judged are *Ptah,* the Egyptian god of life,[39] *Min,* the god of procreation and reproduction, and *Hathor,* one of seven deities who was believed to attend the birth of children. Furthermore, the death of the Apis bull, a firstborn animal with supposedly divine qualities, would have had a tremendous impact on the worshipers and priests of the temple.[40] All the firstborn in Egypt died as an irrefutable demonstration and proof that no god in Egypt had the power to stand against Yahweh, the incomparable and miraculous One.

Following this awful judgment, Pharaoh finally gave in and simply declared to Moses and Aaron that the children of Israel should leave. He made no qualifications and asked for no concessions. He also requested of Moses: "And also bless me" (Exodus 12:32). This is an amazing request, especially in light of the fact that Pharaoh considered himself to be a god. It took ten miraculous plagues, but Yahweh—by means of these plagues—answered the question Pharaoh asked in Exodus 5:2: "Who is the Lord [Yahweh], that I should obey him and let Israel go?"

Many scholars believe the number "ten" represents *completeness,* as seems to be the case with the Ten Commandments (Exodus 20). In the present passage, the occurrence of ten plagues may symbolize the completeness of God's judgment on Egypt.[41] Yahweh left no room for doubt. He alone is God. There is no one like Him. The Pharaoh asked the question. Yahweh answered the question and left no room for misunderstanding: "By this you will know that I am the Lord" (7:5; 7:17; 10:2). *Our miracle-working God prevailed.* The Israelites left Egypt.

Crossing the Red Sea

It was not long before Pharaoh had a change of heart. Letting *that* many slaves go free was intolerable (Exodus 14:5). So Pharaoh called out his troops and led the chase in his chariot. He took with him 600 of Egypt's best chariots. The Egyptian army caught up with the Israelites as they were camped beside the shore of the Red Sea near Pi Hahiroth, across from Baal Zephon (verse 9).

Yahweh's miracles were not over. As Moses stretched out his hand—indicating to all present that what was about to happen was not a natural phenomenon—the Lord split the sea with a strong east wind (Exodus 14:21). This was no shallow body of water. We are not told precisely *how* deep the water was, but it was deep enough that the Egyptian army drowned when God brought the waters back together again (verse 28).

Moreover, we are not speaking of a *narrow* dividing of the water. We don't know precisely *how* wide it was, but it had to be sufficient for over two million Israelites to pass through to the other side along with their flocks and herds.

As God knew would be the case, the Egyptians fully intended to pursue the Israelites with their horses and chariots (Exodus 14:23). During the last watch of the night—between 2 A.M. and 6 A.M.—the Lord (the Angel of Yahweh) looked down from the pillar of fire and cloud at the Egyptian army and threw it into confusion (verse 24). One way He did this was to make the wheels of the Egyptian chariots come off as they pursued the Israelites through the Red Sea.

Psalm 77:16-19 tells us that God caused a rainstorm, lightning, thunder, and an earthquake during this time. It may be that the rain quickly soaked up the sea floor and caused the wheels of the chariots to get stuck and fall off. All of this—combined with the fact that there were two walls of water on each side, caused by a powerful, buffeting east wind—caused the Egyptian soldiers to say: "Let's get away from the Israelites! The LORD is fighting for them against Egypt" (Exodus 14:25). Nevertheless, they were ordered by Pharaoh to pursue the Israelites through the Red Sea.

At daybreak, once the Israelites were on the other side of the Red Sea, Moses stretched out his hand over the sea, and the walls of water collapsed and crushed the Egyptians. Not a single soldier survived (Exodus 14:26-28). *What a mighty miracle this was!*

When the Israelites saw God's great power displayed against the Egyptians, they "feared the LORD and put their trust in him and in Moses his servant" (Exodus 14:30,31). The word *trust* comes from a Hebrew word meaning *to confirm* or *to support*. Through this miraculous deliverance from Egypt and then the miraculous Red Sea experience, the Israelites came to support Moses as God's representative.

Some critics have denied the historicity of the Red Sea miracle. Some suggest there was no supernatural wind caused by God, but rather a strong *natural* wind accounted for what took place. Another critic has suggested there was a volcanic eruption that sent a strong windblast across the land that temporarily separated the Red Sea. Others have suggested the Israelites crossed a shallow area of the Red Sea.

Such suggestions fail to do justice to the biblical data. First, if the Israelites crossed at a shallow part of the Red Sea, then (as noted previously) how did the highly trained Egyptian soldiers drown (Exodus 14:28; 15:4,5)? A strong natural wind couldn't have caused this phenomenon because the natural winds in this area flow *north* and *south*; the wind that separated the Red Sea blew from the east— something that is completely *un*natural. It is also impossible that a natural wind could have created two walls of water that ran through the Red Sea. Moreover, a single blast from a volcano cannot explain what happened because the separation of the Red Sea had to last long enough for over two million people to cross. (And besides, a volcano blast would have incinerated the Israelites.) Clearly, what happened at the Red Sea was a supernatural miracle. All other explanations fail.

Entrance into the Promised Land

At the end of the wilderness journey, long after the deliverance from Egypt, Moses offered a prayer to God concerning Israel's long-anticipated entrance into the promised land. Based on his past experiences (recorded in Exodus), Moses proclaimed, "O sovereign LORD, you have begun to show to your servant your greatness and your strong hand. For what god is there in heaven or on earth who can do the deeds and mighty works you do?" (Deuteronomy 3:24).

Following this prayer, Moses set out to provide instructions to the nation of Israel before they entered the promised land. Part of his goal was to instill faithfulness in the Israelites so they would not turn their backs on Yahweh. This admonition climaxes in Deuteronomy 4:34, 35, and 39:

> Has any god ever tried to take for himself one nation out of another nation, by testings, by miraculous signs and wonders, by war, by a mighty hand and an outstretched arm, or by great and awesome deeds, like all the things the LORD your God did for you in Egypt before your very eyes? You were shown these things so that you might know that the LORD is God; besides him there is no other.... Acknowledge and take to heart this day that the LORD is God in heaven above and on the earth below. There is no other.

The comparative question in verse 34 is aimed at stressing the fact of Yahweh's *in*comparability, which in turn demonstrates His utter uniqueness. Reflecting on past events, Moses compared Yahweh with other gods and concluded that, since no other god had ever attempted what Yahweh did, Yahweh alone is incomparable.[42] Indeed, since no other god had ever attempted what Yahweh did, such so-called gods are really nonentities. There is only one God—and He is the miracle-working God of the Bible!

Points to Ponder

- True miracles exalt the one true God, not false gods, and not human beings.

- If you become aware of a miracle claim associated with a false religious system (such as a cult), you may be certain it is *not* a miracle of God.

- If you become aware of alleged miraculous phenomena in which a human being puts on a show and exalts himself instead of God, you may assume this is not of God.

- "Miracles" associated with false religions often involve conjuring tricks that are not true miracles. (An example would be modern psychic healers that feign removing a diseased organ from a person's body.) *Beware!*

~

FIVE

The Miracle of the Incarnation

C. S. Lewis once said "the central miracle asserted by Christians is the Incarnation....Every other miracle prepares for this, or exhibits this, or results from this." Indeed, the incarnation is "the Grand Miracle."[1] Renowned Bible scholar Merrill Tenney likewise asserted that the "stupendous miracle of the Incarnation" is at the very heart of the message of Scripture.[2] Gene Getz affirmed that "one of the most profound truths in the Word of God is the miracle of the Incarnation—God's Son became a complete man while remaining genuinely God."[3] Carl F. Henry likewise declared that "the New Testament revolves about the miraculous incarnation of God in Jesus Christ and about his supernatural resurrection from the dead."[4] Kenneth O. Gangel points us to the fact that "in the miracle of creation, God made man. In the miracle of the Incarnation, He gave man the *God-man*."[5]

In the incarnation, the incomprehensible came to pass. The glorious Son of God forsook the splendor of heaven and became as genuinely human as we ourselves are. Surrendering His glorious estate, He voluntarily entered into human relationships within the world of time and space. "Leaving the free, unconditioned, world-ruling absoluteness of the divine form, the Son entered the limits of time and space of the creature."[6] Jesus became a man, was crucified on a cross, rose from the dead as the glorified God-man, and ascended back into His original glory. All of this He did for our sake.

The incarnation is not an easy doctrine. When pondering the great truth that in the incarnation Christ as eternal God* took on a human nature, we are immediately faced with a deluge of mind-boggling questions. For example, how could Christ be both fully human *and* fully divine at the same time? What is the relationship between the human and divine natures in Christ? Do the two natures merge to form a third compound nature, or do they remain forever distinct? Did Christ in His two natures have two wills or just one will? Did Christ have conflicting desires—some human and some divine? Did Christ give up any of His divine attributes during His incarnate state? Was Christ *still* human following His death and resurrection?

These are difficult questions. But they are questions that the Scriptures address, in varying degrees of detail. In this chapter, we shall focus our attention on these and other issues related to the grand miracle of the incarnation.

The Humanity of Christ

To deny either the undiminished deity *or* the perfect humanity of Christ in the incarnation is to put oneself out-

---

*Scripture is clear that Christ is eternal God. Divine names are ascribed to Him, such as "God" (Hebrews 1:8), "Lord" (Matthew 22:43-45), and "King of kings and Lord of lords" (Revelation 19:16). He has all the divine attributes, including eternality (Micah 5:2), omnipotence (Matthew 28:18), omniscience (John 1:48), and omnipresence (Matthew 18:20). He did things only God can do, such as creating the universe (John 1:3) and raising people from the dead (John 5:25;11). He is also worshiped as God—by both human beings (Matthew 14:33) and angels (Hebrews 1:6).

side the pale of orthodoxy.[7] First John 4:2,3 tells us: "This is how you can recognize the Spirit of God: Every spirit that acknowledges that Jesus Christ has come in the flesh is from God, but every spirit that does not acknowledge Jesus is not from God. This is the spirit of the antichrist, which you have heard is coming and even now is already in the world."

Innumerable passages in the New Testament confirm Christ's full humanity in the incarnation. Hebrews 2:14 tells us, for example, that since His children "have flesh and blood, he too shared in their humanity so that by his death he might destroy him who holds the power of death—that is, the devil." First Timothy 3:16 affirms that Jesus "appeared in a body, was vindicated by the Spirit, was seen by angels, was preached among the nations, was believed on in the world, was taken up in glory." Romans 8:3 says that God sent Jesus "in the likeness of sinful man to be a sin offering."

Normal Fetal Growth and Birth

While remaining fully God within the womb, as a human being Jesus experienced a normal fetal state, had an umbilical cord through which He received sustenance to His human body from His mother Mary, developed for nine months in the womb, and experienced a natural human birth. As Bible scholar Robert Gromacki puts it, "Apart from the virgin conception and overshadowing ministry of the Holy Spirit, Mary's pregnancy was no different than that of any other human mother."[8]

It is important to grasp that it was the *conception* of Jesus in Mary's womb that was supernatural, not His *birth* (see Isaiah 7:14; Luke 1:35; 2:6,7). The miraculous conception that resulted from the overshadowing ministry of the Holy Spirit (Luke 1:35) made it possible for the preexistent, eternal Son to take on a human nature through Mary.

Normal Human Development

Scripture is clear that even though Jesus never for a moment surrendered any aspect of His deity, He experienced normal human development through infancy, childhood, adolescence, and into adulthood. According to Luke 2:40, Jesus "grew," "became strong," and was "filled with wisdom." These are things that could never be said of Jesus' divine nature. It was in His humanity that He grew, became strong, and became filled with wisdom.

Likewise, Luke 2:52 tells us that "Jesus grew in wisdom and stature." Again, Jesus' growth in wisdom and stature is something that can only be said of His humanity. Many scholars have noted that Jesus' expert use of the Old Testament Scriptures during His three-year ministry was due to His "growth in wisdom" as He studied the Old Testament while growing up.[9] Bible scholar Edgar J. Goodspeed comments:

> No wonder Jesus could use [the writings of the Hebrew prophets] with such power in his brief ministry; he had studied and pondered them for many years, as no one has ever done, before or since. It is customary to dismiss his mastery of what was basic in them as simply effortless revelation, as though he just knew all about their meaning all the time, because he was himself; but that is not the picture of the gospels. He had to *grow*, as Luke is careful to say, in wisdom as well as stature.[10]

Christ's development as a human being was normal in every respect, with two major exceptions: 1) Christ always did the will of God; and 2) He never sinned. As Hebrews 4:15 tells us, in Christ "we do not have a high priest who is unable to sympathize with our weaknesses, but we have one who has been tempted in every way, just as we are—yet was without sin." Indeed, Christ is "holy," "blameless," and "pure" (Hebrews 7:26). Hence, though Christ was utterly sinless, His human nature was exactly the same as ours in every other respect.[11]

Jesus' full humanity is plainly evident in the fact that He consistently displayed human characteristics. Besides growing as a normal child (Luke 2:40,52), Jesus had a physical body of flesh and bones (Luke 24:39), experienced weariness (John 4:6), hunger (Luke 4:2), sorrow (Matthew 26:37), weeping (John 11:35), and needed sleep (Luke 8:23).

Scripture is also clear that Christ possessed a fully human spirit and soul. For example, John 11:33 describes the emotion Jesus felt in His human *spirit* when His friend Lazarus died. At the prospect of His impending crucifixion, Jesus was troubled in His *soul* (John 12:27) and in His *spirit* (John 13:21). When He died on the cross, He gave up His *spirit* to the Father (John 19:30). In view of these Scriptures, theologian John F. Walvoord rightly concludes that

> Christ possessed a true humanity not only in its material aspects as indicated in His human body, but in the immaterial aspect specified in Scripture as being His soul and spirit. It is therefore not sufficient to recognize that Jesus Christ as the Son of God possessed a human body, but is necessary to view Him as having a complete human nature including body, soul, and spirit.[12]

Jesus Affirmed His Humanity

On a number of occasions, Jesus referred to His humanity in very clear terms. For example, recall that when He was tempted by Satan, Jesus responded with the words: "Man does not live on bread alone, but on every word that comes from the mouth of God" (Matthew 4:4). Jesus was here applying to Himself Deuteronomy 8:3, a passage that in its original context was written regarding *man's* relationship to God. On another occasion, Jesus told some angry Jews who were trying to kill Him: "You are determined to kill me, a man who has told you the truth that I heard from God" (John 8:40).[13]

Jesus' human nature was certainly recognized by others. One example of this is found in Acts 2:22, in which we find Peter preaching his Pentecost sermon. In this sermon, Peter said: "Men of Israel, listen to this: Jesus of Nazareth was a *man* accredited by God to you by miracles, wonders and signs, which God did among you through him, as you yourselves know" (emphasis added). The apostle Paul provides another example in his assertion that "there is one God and one mediator between God and men, the *man* Christ Jesus, who gave himself as a ransom for all men" (1 Timothy 2:5, emphasis added).

Hence, though Jesus was (is) fully and eternally God, He took on a *fully* human nature through the miracle of the incarnation. We are neither more nor less human than He was. When His hands, feet, and side were pierced, blood came out of the wounds—just as it would have been for us.

Condescension and Exaltation: Philippians 2:6-9

If Jesus Christ is in fact God, as Scripture emphatically declares, then how does His deity relate to His humanity? This question is dealt with in Philippians 2:6-9. Paul, speaking of the miraculous incarnation, says that Christ, "being in very nature God, did not consider equality with God something to be grasped, but made himself nothing, taking the very nature of a servant, being made in human likeness" (verses 6,7).

Paul's affirmation that Christ was "in very nature God" is extremely significant. Christ in His essential being *is* and *always has been* eternal God—just as much as the Father and the Holy Spirit. Theologian Charles Ryrie notes that the word *nature* in the Greek connotes "that which is intrinsic and essential to the thing. Thus here it means that our Lord in His preincarnate state possessed essential deity."[14] Reformed theologian Benjamin Warfield comments that the word *nature* "is a term which expresses the sum of those characterizing qualities which make a thing the precise thing that it is."[15] Used of God, the word refers to "the sum of the characteristics which make the being we call 'God,' specifically God, rather than some other being—an angel, say, or a man."[16]

It is noteworthy that the word *being* (in the phrase, "being in very nature God") is a present-tense participle and carries the idea of *continued existence* as God.[17] Here the thought is that Christ always has been in the form of God with the implication that He still is.[18] Theologian Robert Reymond notes that "when we take into account the force of the present participle, which conveys the idea of 'continually [beforehand] subsisting' (which in turn excludes any intimation that this mode of subsistence came to an end when He assumed the form of servant), we have here as bold and unqualified an assertion of both the preexistence and the full and unabridged deity of Jesus Christ as one could ever hope to find in the pages of the New Testament."[19] Thus this verse indicates that Jesus Christ, in eternity past, continually and forever existed in the form of God, outwardly manifesting His divine attributes. *This* is the one who was born from the womb of Mary as a human being, all the while retaining His full deity. *This* is the miracle of the incarnation.

Having said all this about Christ's essential deity, a key question remains: In what way did Christ make Himself "nothing" when He became incarnate (Philippians 2:7)? This question has been debated down through the centuries, and the debate will no doubt continue until the second coming. Space limitations do not allow for an in-depth study of this issue. The following brief summary is sufficient for our purposes.

The Veiling of Christ's Preincarnate Glory

Paul's statement that Christ made Himself "nothing" in the incarnation involves three basic issues: the veiling of His preincarnate glory, a voluntary nonuse of some of His divine attributes on some occasions, and the condescension involved in taking on the likeness of human beings.

One thing is certain, however. This *does not* mean that Jesus gave up His deity. Indeed, this is impossible, since God cannot cease to be God.

Regarding the veiling of Christ's preincarnate glory, Scripture indicates that it was necessary for Christ to give up the *outer appearance* of God in order to take upon Himself the form of man. Of course, Christ never actually *surrendered* His divine glory. Recall that on the Mount of Transfiguration (prior to His crucifixion), Jesus allowed His intrinsic glory to shine forth for a brief time, illuminating the whole mountainside (Matthew 17). Nevertheless, it was necessary for Jesus to *veil* His preincarnate glory in order to dwell among mortal men.

Had Christ *not* veiled His preincarnate glory, humankind would not have been able to behold Him. It would have been the same as when the apostle John, more than 50 years after Christ's resurrection, beheld Christ in His glory and said: "I fell at his feet as though dead" (Revelation 1:17); or as when Isaiah beheld the glory of Christ in his vision in the temple and said, "Woe to me!...I am ruined" (Isaiah 6:5; see John 12:41).

Christ's Voluntary Nonuse of Some Divine Attributes

A second issue involved in Christ making Himself "nothing" in the miraculous incarnation had to do with submission to a *voluntary nonuse of some of His divine attributes on some occasions* in order for Him to accomplish His objectives. Christ could never have actually *surrendered* any of His attributes, for then He would have ceased to be God.[20] But He could (and did) voluntarily cease using some of them on some occasions during His time on earth (approximately 4 B.C. to A.D. 29) in order to live among people and their limitations.

Though Christ sometimes chose not to use His divine attributes, at other times He *did* use them. For example, on different occasions during His three-year ministry, Jesus exercised the divine attributes of *omniscience* (that is, all-knowingness—John 2:24; 16:30), *omnipresence* (being everywhere-present—John 1:48), and *omnipotence* (being all-powerful, as evidenced by His many miracles—John 11). Hence, whatever limitations Christ may have suffered when He "made himself nothing" (Philippians 2:7), He did not subtract a single divine attribute from Himself or in any sense make Himself less than God.

One of the divine attributes is known in theological circles as "immutability," which refers to the fact that God cannot change in His nature or essence. This attribute is expressly affirmed of Christ in Hebrews 13:8. As such, it is clear that Christ, as God, cannot change in His essential being, and hence He could never give up any of His divine attributes. Indeed, as Walvoord puts it, "God cannot change His nature by act of His will any more than any other being. Attributes inherent in a personal essence cannot be dismissed."[21] All of Christ's divine attributes are His *eternal* possession and continued in the incarnate state.[22]

The question that arises at this point is, *Why* did Jesus choose on occasion not to use some of His divine attributes? It would seem that Christ submitted to a voluntary nonuse of some of His attributes in keeping with His purpose of living among human beings and their limitations. He does not seem to have ever used His divine attributes on His own behalf, though certainly His attributes were gloriously displayed in the many miracles He performed for others.

To be more specific, the scriptural testimony indicates that Christ never used His omniscience to make His own life as a human being easier. He suffered all the inconveniences of His day despite the fact that in His divine omniscience He had infinite awareness of every human device ever conceived for human comfort.[23]

Nor did Christ use His omnipotence or omnipresence to make His life as a human easier. Though Jesus as God could have, in His omnipotence, just willed Himself from Bethany to Jerusalem, and He would have been instantly there, He instead traveled by foot like every other human and experienced fatigue in the process. Of course, as God, Christ in His divine nature (with His attribute of omnipresence) was in both Bethany and Jerusalem at the same time. But He voluntarily chose not to use this attribute on those occasions during His three-year ministry that would have made His life as a human being easier. In a word, then, Jesus restricted the benefits of His divine attributes as they pertained to His walk on earth and of His own accord chose not to use His powers to lift Himself above ordinary human limitations.[24]

Christ's Condescension

A third issue involved in Christ making Himself "nothing" in the miraculous incarnation had to do with His condescending by taking on the *likeness* (literally "form" or "appearance") of humans, and taking on the *form* ("essence" or "nature") of a bondservant.[25] Christ was thus truly human.

This humanity was one that was subject to temptation, distress, weakness, pain, sorrow, and limitation.[26] Yet at the same time it must be noted that the word *likeness* suggests similarity *but difference.* As theologian Robert Lightner explains, "though His humanity was genuine, He was different from all other humans in that He was sinless."[27] Nevertheless, Christ's taking on the likeness of humans represented a great *condescension* on the part of the second person of the Trinity.

Theologians have been careful to point out that the incarnation involved a gaining of *human* attributes and not a giving up of *divine* attributes. That this is indeed meant by Paul is clear in his affirmation that in the incarnation Christ was "taking the very nature of a servant," "being made in human likeness," and "being found in appearance as a man" (Philippians 2:7,8). J. I. Packer says Jesus was no less God in the incarnation than before, but He had begun to be man. "He was not now God *minus* some elements of His deity, but God *plus* all that He had made His own by taking manhood to Himself. He who *made* man was now learning what it felt like to *be* man."[28] In other words, it was not the subtraction of deity but the addition of humanity. *This* is the miracle of the incarnation.

The Union of the Human and Divine Natures in Christ

How infinite God and finite humanity can be united in one single person is one of the most difficult of all theological problems. It ranks in complexity with the Trinity and the paradox of divine sovereignty versus human free will. The secret of Christ's self-humbling is forever unfathomable. It transcends human reason.[29] It is a miracle that boggles the mind. Nevertheless, Scripture provides us with some intriguing facts about this inscrutable union. The remainder of this chapter will summarize these facts.

What is a Nature?

Crucial to a proper understanding of the incarnation is grasping what is meant by the word *nature*. This word is commonly used to designate the divine or human elements in the person of Christ. In other words, *nature* when used of Christ's divinity refers to all that belongs to deity, including all the attributes of deity. *Nature* when used of Christ's humanity refers to all that belongs to humanity, including all the attributes of humanity. Another way to describe *nature* is that it refers to "the sum-total of all the essential qualities of a thing, that which makes it what it is."[30]

The Incarnate Christ: One Person

Though the incarnate Christ had both a human and a divine nature, He was only one person—as indicated by His consistent use of "I," "me," and "mine" in reference to Himself. Jesus never used the words "us," "we," or "ours" in reference to His human-divine person. Nor did the divine nature of Christ ever carry on a verbal conversation with His human nature.

This is completely unlike the doctrine of the Trinity. The persons in the Godhead use personal pronouns of each other—that is, the Father says "you" to the Son, and the Son says "you" to the Father. And when God created man, He said "Let *us* make man in *our* image" (Genesis 1:26, emphasis added). This is because there are three persons within the Godhead. Therefore, as Robert Gromacki notes, "there is no direct analogy between the Trinitarian oneness of God and the *theanthropic* [God-Man] person of Christ. In the former, there are three persons but only one nature, *divine;*

in the latter there is only one person with two natures, *human* and *divine.*"[31]

Hence, the eternal Son of God—who, prior to the incarnation, was one in person and nature (wholly divine)—became, in the miraculous incarnation, *two* in nature (divine and human) while remaining *one* person. The Son, who had already been a person for all eternity past, joined Himself not with a human *person* but with a human *nature* at the incarnation.[32]

An Inscrutable Mystery

One of the most complex aspects of the relationship of Christ's two natures is that, while the attributes of one nature are never attributed to the other, the attributes of both natures are properly attributed to His one person. Thus Christ at the same moment in time had what seem to be contradictory qualities. He was finite and yet infinite, weak and yet omnipotent, increasing in knowledge and yet omniscient, limited to being in one place at one time and yet omnipresent. In the incarnation, the person of Christ is the partaker of the attributes of both natures, so that whatever may be affirmed of either nature—human or divine—may be affirmed of the one person.

Though Christ sometimes operated in the sphere of His humanity and in other cases in the sphere of His deity, in all cases what He did and what He was could be attributed to His one person. Thus, though Christ in His human nature knew hunger (Luke 4:2), weariness (John 4:6), and the need for sleep (Luke 8:23), just as Christ in His divine nature was omniscient (John 2:24), omnipresent (John 1:48), and omnipotent (John 11), *all of this was experienced by the one person of Jesus Christ.*

The Human-Divine Union Lasts Forever

When Christ became a man in the incarnation, He did not enter into a temporary union of the human and divine natures that ended at His death. Rather, Scripture is clear that Christ's human nature continues forever. The miracle of the incarnation is a *forever* miracle.

Christ was raised immortal in the very same human body in which He died (Luke 24:37-39; Acts 2:31; 1 John 4:2; 2 John 7). When Christ ascended into heaven, He ascended in the same physical human body, as witnessed by several of His disciples (Acts 1:11). When Christ returns, He will return as the "Son of Man"—a messianic title that points to His humanity (Matthew 26:64). At the same time, even though Jesus has fully retained His humanity and will return as the glorified God-man, the glory that He now has in heaven is no less than the resplendent glory that has been His *as God* for all eternity past (see John 17:5).

The Death of the God-Man

If Christ forever retained His humanity following the crucifixion, then what precisely occurred when Christ the God-man died on the cross? To answer this question, we must note that the Greek word for death *(thanatos)* conveys the idea of separation. When a person dies physically, his immaterial nature (soul and spirit) separates from his physical body. When Jesus died on the cross, the divine person with His divine nature *and* with His human immaterial nature (soul and spirit) departed from His human body. *There was no separation of the divine nature from the human nature in the person of Jesus when He died.* Christ was just as much a human being *after* His death as He was before. Then at the resurrection, Christ's real self, including His divine nature and His immaterial human nature, was joined to the same physical (human) body in which He died, now immortal and incorruptible.

At the incarnation, then, the person of Christ became eternally wedded to a human nature. He did not discard any part of His humanity at His death, resurrection, or ascension.

The Relation of the Human and Divine Natures

How could two different natures—one infinite and one finite—exist within one person? Would not one nature be dominated by the other? Would not each nature be forced to surrender some of its qualities in order for each to coexist beside each other? Could Jesus be *truly God* and *truly man* simultaneously?[33]

In the early history of the church, there was much confusion regarding how such incompatible natures could be joined in one person without one or the other losing some of its essential characteristics. The discussion that resulted from this confusion, however, led to the orthodox statement that the two natures are united without mixture and without loss of any essential attributes, and that the two natures maintain their separate identities without transfer of any property or attribute of one nature to the other.[34] As theologian Robert Lightner puts it,

> In the union of the human and divine in Christ each of the natures retained its own attributes. Deity did not permeate humanity, nor did humanity become absorbed into deity. The two natures retain their complete identity even though they have been joined together in a personal union. Christ is thus *theanthropic* (God-man) in person. Embracing perfect humanity made Him no less God, and retaining His undiminished deity did not make Him less human.[35]

In the joining of the human and divine natures in one person, it is critical to recognize that there was no mixture to form a third compound nature. The human nature always remained human, and the divine nature always remained divine. To divest the divine nature of God of a single attribute would destroy His deity, and to divest man of a single human attribute would result in the destruction of a true humanity. It is for this reason that the two natures of Christ cannot lose or transfer a single attribute.[36] The two natures remain distinct.

Along these lines, the Chalcedonian Creed affirms that the two natures were united *without mixture, without change, without division,* and *without separation.*[37] Hence, the miraculous union of the two natures in Christ should not be thought of as deity merely possessing humanity, for this would deny true humanity its rightful place. On the other hand, the incarnation was not merely humanity indwelt by deity. In Christ's unique personality He possessed two natures, one eternal and divine, the other human and generated in time.[38]

Christ must therefore be seen as a "theanthropic" person. We noted earlier that "theanthropic" means "God-man." This word is actually a compound that combines two Greek words: *theos* (meaning "God") and *anthropos* (meaning "man"). Jesus is the *Theos-anthropos,* the God-man.

Christ, however, did not have a theanthropic *nature* that resulted from a merging of the divine and human natures in Him. We must stress that Christ in the incarnation was neither a divine man nor a human God. He is the "God-man," *fully God* and *fully man.* He is no less God because of His humanity and no less human because of His deity.[39] *This* is the miracle of the incarnation.

The Relation of the Two Natures to the Self-Consciousness of Christ

As God, Jesus during His incarnate state was always aware of His deity. His divine self-consciousness was as fully operative when He was a babe in Mary's arms in Bethlehem as it was in His most mature experience as an adult.

But what about a human self-consciousness? In his book *Jesus Christ Our Lord,* John F. Walvoord notes that there is evidence that

> the human nature developed and with it a human self-consciousness came into play.... It seems possible to conclude that He had both a divine and a human self-consciousness, that these were never in conflict, and that Christ sometimes thought, spoke, and acted from the divine self-consciousness and at other times from the human.[40]

It seems legitimate to conclude, then, that Jesus in the incarnation was *one* person with *two* different kinds of consciousness—a divine consciousness and a human consciousness. In His divine consciousness He could say, "I and the Father are one" (John 10:30), "Before Abraham was born, I am" (John 8:58), and "I am the way and the truth and the life. No one comes to the Father except through me" (John 14:6). In His human consciousness Jesus could make such statements as, "I am thirsty" (John 19:28).

The Relation of the Two Natures to the Will(s) of Christ

If Christ had two kinds of consciousness, did He also have two wills? The Council of Chalcedon said that Christ had two natures united in one person, thus implying two wills. An examination of the Gospels indicates that every single decision and action of Christ stemmed from either His divine nature or from His human nature—or, in some cases, a blending of both. In view of this, it may be proper to think of Christ as having two wills. Theologian William G. T. Shedd says that "each nature, in order to be whole and entire, must have all of its essential elements. A human nature without voluntariness would be as defective as it would be without rationality."[41] However, since both actions stem from one person *(will-er),* it is correct to speak of one will in Christ. In short, Christ's will was one in *source* (he was one person) but two in *manifestation* (through His two natures).

Two Spheres of Activity—Human and Divine

The Gospel accounts are clear that Christ operated at different times under the major influence of one or the other of His two natures. Indeed, Christ operated in the human sphere to the extent that it was necessary for Him to accomplish His earthly purpose as determined in the eternal plan of salvation. At the same time, He operated in the divine sphere to the extent that it was possible in the period of His humiliation.

It is interesting that both of Christ's natures come into play in many events recorded in the Gospels. For example, Christ's initial approach to the fig tree to pick and eat a fig to relieve His hunger reflected the natural ignorance of the human mind (Matthew 21:19a). (That is, in His humanity He did not know from a distance that there was no fruit on that particular tree.) But then He immediately revealed His divine omnipotence by causing the tree to wither (verse 19b).

On another occasion, Jesus in His omniscience knew that His friend Lazarus had died, and he set off for Bethany (John 11:11). When Jesus arrived in Bethany, He asked (in His humanness, without exercising omniscience) where

Lazarus had been laid (verse 34). Theologian Robert Reymond notes that as the God-man, Jesus is "simultaneously omniscient as God (in company with the other persons of the Godhead) and ignorant of some things as man (in company with the other persons of the human race)."[42]

Important Results of the Human-Divine Union

One could write an entire book on the important results of the miraculous human-divine union in the person of Christ. I will offer only a brief summary here, focusing on Christ as Redeemer and High Priest.

Christ Our Redeemer

Humankind's redemption was completely dependent upon the miraculous human-divine union in Christ. If Christ the Redeemer had been *only* God, He could not have died, since God by His very nature cannot die. It was only as a man that Christ could represent humanity and die as a man. As God, however, Christ's death had infinite value, sufficient to provide redemption for the sins of all humankind. Clearly, then, Christ had to be both God *and* man to secure man's salvation (1 Timothy 2:5).

This is related to the Old Testament concept of the kinsman-redeemer. In Old Testament times, the phrase *kinsman-redeemer* was always used of one who was related by blood to someone he was seeking to redeem from bondage. If someone was sold into slavery, for example, it was the duty of a blood relative—the "next of kin"—to act as that person's "kinsman-redeemer" and buy him out of slavery (Leviticus 25:47,48).

Jesus is the Kinsman-Redeemer for sin-enslaved humanity. For Jesus to become a Kinsman-Redeemer, however, He had to become related *by blood* to the human race. This indicates the necessity of the incarnation. Jesus became a man in order to redeem man (Hebrews 2:14-16). And because Jesus was also fully God, His sacrificial death had infinite value (9:11-28).

Christ Our Priest

Christ's human-divine union also enabled Him to become our eternal High Priest. Through the incarnation, Christ became a man and hence could act as a human priest. As God, Christ's priesthood could be everlasting and perfect in every way.

Because the divine Christ became a man in the incarnation, He as our Priest is able to intercede in prayer for us. Since Jesus was truly one of us, experiencing all of the temptations and trials of human existence, He is fully able to understand and empathize with us in our struggles as human beings. Hebrews 4:15,16 tells us "we do not have a high priest who is unable to sympathize with our weaknesses, but we have one who has been tempted in every way, just as we are—yet was without sin. Let us then approach the throne of grace with confidence, so that we may receive mercy and find grace to help us in our time of need."

If Christ was *not* human, or only *incompletely* human, then He would not have been able to make the kind of intercession a priest must make on behalf of those whom He represents. Because Christ is fully human *and* fully God, "he is able to save completely those who come to God through him, because he always lives to intercede for them" (Hebrews 7:25).

Even now, Christ—the glorified God-man in His heavenly abode—is interceding on our behalf on an individual, personal basis. He knows each of us intimately, including all our weaknesses, temptations, and human failings. How reassuring it is that Christ, who is completely familiar with what it is like to be a human, prays for us specifically according to our need. Praise be to our eternal God, Savior, Redeemer, and High Priest, Jesus Christ! *Praise God for the miracle of the incarnation!*

Points to Ponder

- The incarnation is a one-time miracle, never to be repeated.

- If you see a cult leader today claiming to be the new "incarnation" of Christ, this is a *false* miracle claim. This is *not* God at work.

- If you encounter a book—such as the New Age *Course in Miracles*—that says all human beings are an "incarnation" of the Christ, this is a *false* miracle claim. This is *not* God at work.

- Ponder Jesus' words in Matthew 24:4-6.

SIX

~

The Miracles
of Jesus

Scripture often refers to the miracles of Jesus as "signs."
As noted previously in the book, this word emphasizes
the *significance* of the action rather than the *marvel* of
it (see John 4:54; 6:14; 9:16). These signs were strategically
performed by Jesus to *signify* His true identity and glory as
the divine Messiah.

This is illustrated in the account of John the Baptist in
jail. After being locked up, John sent his disciples to ask
Jesus, "Are you the one who was to come, or should we
expect someone else?" (Matthew 11:2,3). As a backdrop to
understanding John's question, it was the common viewpoint among the Jews of that time that when the Messiah
came, He would set up His glorious kingdom. There were
very high messianic expectations in the first century, and
even John himself probably expected the soon emergence of
the kingdom he himself had been preaching about.

But now something unexpected happened—*John was
imprisoned.* Instead of the kingdom, which (it was commonly
thought) would be characterized by such things as liberty
and freedom, John now found himself locked up in jail and

in danger of execution. So—what was John to make of this development? John may have expected Jesus to use more coercive powers as the Messiah/deliverer of Israel. He thus decided to send messengers to ask Jesus, "Are you the one who was to come, or should we expect someone else?" (Luke 7:20).

Jesus' response is extremely significant. Instead of merely giving verbal assurance that He was in fact the divine Messiah, He pointed to His miraculous acts, including giving sight to the blind, enabling the lame to walk, and opening deaf ears (Luke 7:22). Why did Jesus do this? Because these were the precise miracles prophesied to be performed by the Messiah when He came (see Isaiah 29:18-21; 35:5,6; 61:1,2). The miraculous deeds alone ("signs") were more than enough proof that Jesus was the promised Messiah. The miracles were Jesus' divine credentials—His divine "ID Card," so to speak.

There is another point that bears mentioning. Jesus' choice to avoid coming right out and saying, "You can rest assured I am the Messiah," may have been because of the popular misconceptions of the Messiah among the masses (and perhaps even John himself). It may be that Jesus' intention in sending the messengers to report about His miracles was to indicate to John, "Yes, I am the Messiah—the *true* Messiah prophesied in the Old Testament, who will deliver people from bondage to sin and be verified by mighty miracles—but not the Messiah of popular misconception, the coercive political deliverer so many are expecting today."

John's Gospel tells us that Jesus' signs were performed in the presence of His disciples to ensure that there was adequate witness to the events that transpired (John 20:30). "Witness" is a pivotal concept in this Gospel. The noun ("witness") is used 14 times and the verb ("testify") 33 times, and the reason for this is clear. *The signs performed by Jesus are thoroughly attested.* There were many witnesses. Therefore, the signs cannot be simply dismissed or explained away!

Thirty-five separate miracles performed by Christ are recorded in the Gospels. Of these, Matthew mentioned 20; Mark, 18; Luke, 20; and John, 7. But these are only a selection from among many that He did (Matthew 4:23,24; 11:4,5; 21:14). The miracles or signs that are recorded in Scripture are presented "that you may believe that Jesus is the Christ, the Son of God" (John 20:31). "The Christ" is used in this verse in the sense of a title rather than a name. It means "Anointed One," and was a common term used of the Messiah among the Jews. Scripture presents indisputable evidence *in the signs* (or miracles) that Jesus is the Christ and the Son of God.

John's Gospel goes on to tell us "Jesus did many other things as well. If every one of them were written down, I suppose that even the whole world would not have room for the books that would be written" (John 21:25). Among the many miracles attributed to Jesus in the New Testament are: changing water into wine (John 2:7,8); healing the nobleman's son (John 4:50); healing the Capernaum demoniac (Mark 1:25; Luke 4:35); healing Peter's mother-in-law (Matthew 8:15; Mark 1:31; Luke 4:39); causing the disciples to catch a great number of fish (Luke 5:5,6); healing a leper (Matthew 8:3; Mark 1:41); healing a paralytic (Matthew 9:2; Mark 2:5; Luke 5:20); healing a withered hand (Matthew 12:13; Mark 3:5; Luke 6:10); healing a centurion's servant (Matthew 8:13; Luke 7:10); raising a widow's son (Luke 7:14); calming a stormy sea (Matthew 8:26; Mark 4:39; Luke 8:24); healing the Gadarene demoniac (Matthew 8:32; Mark 5:8; Luke 8:33); healing a woman with internal bleeding (Matthew 9:22; Mark 5:29; Luke 8:44); raising Jairus's daughter (Matthew 9:25; Mark 5:41; Luke 8:54); healing two blind men (Matthew 9:29); healing a dumb demoniac (Matthew 9:33); healing an invalid (John 5:8); feeding 5000

men and their families (Matthew 14:19; Mark 6:41; Luke
9:16; John 6:11); walking on the sea (Matthew 14:25; Mark
6:48; John 6:19); healing a demoniac girl (Matthew 15:28;
Mark 7:29); healing a deaf man with a speech impediment
(Mark 7:34,35); feeding 4000 men and their families
(Matthew 15:36; Mark 8:6); healing a blind man (Mark
8:25); healing another man born blind (John 9:7); healing
a demoniac boy (Matthew 17:18; Mark 9:25; Luke 9:42);
causing Peter to catch a fish with a coin in its mouth
(Matthew 17:27); healing a blind and dumb demoniac
(Matthew 12:22; Luke 11:14); healing a woman with an 18-
year infirmity (Luke 13:10-17); healing a man with dropsy
(Luke 14:4); healing ten lepers (Luke 17:11-19); raising
Lazarus from the dead (John 11:43,44); healing another
blind man (Matthew 20:34; Luke 18:42); healing yet another
blind man (Matthew 20:34; Mark 10:46); destroying a fig
tree (Matthew 21:19; Mark 11:14); and restoring (healing)
a severed ear (Matthew 26:51; Mark 14:47; Luke 22:50,51;
John 18:10). No wonder Peter would later preach to the Jews
that Jesus was "a man attested to you by God with *mighty works
and wonders and signs* which God did through him in your
midst" (Acts 2:22 emphasis added).

It is not my goal to examine every miracle or "sign" performed by Jesus. (I could write an entire book on this
alone.) But I will look at three *kinds* of signs that clearly attest
to His identity. These are things no mere human could
accomplish.

1. Jesus Controlled the Realm of Nature

In the Gospels, Jesus repeatedly displayed a power over
natural forces that could belong only to God, the author of
these forces. This should not surprise us, for Christ Himself
is the Creator: "For by him all things were created: things in
heaven and on earth, visible and invisible, whether thrones

or powers or rulers or authorities; all things were created by him and for him" (Colossians 1:16). "Through him all things were made; without him nothing was made that has been made" (John 1:3; see also Hebrews 1:2). We should fully expect Christ to exercise control over that which He Himself brought into being.

This is illustrated for us at a wedding banquet in Galilee where Jesus had some servants fill six stone water jars—each holding 20 to 30 gallons—and turned the water (over 120 gallons) into wine (John 2:1-11). "This, the first of his miraculous signs, Jesus performed at Cana in Galilee. He thus revealed his glory, and his disciples put their faith in him" (verse 11). This miracle revealed Jesus as the Creator and disclosed His power over the chemical processes of nature. By a single word of command He accomplished the transformation that a vine requires several months to produce. As theologian Charles Ryrie points out, this miracle

> was accomplished in a moment, without grapes, sun, or time. Of course, it was a miracle that contained the appearance of age. The wine seemed to have come from grapes that grew and matured and were picked and pressed over a period of time. The actual age of the wine was only minutes; the apparent age was a season of growth and harvest.[1]

Shortly thereafter, Jesus multiplied five small loaves of bread and two small fish into enough food to satisfy over 5000 people. Matthew's Gospel indicates those who partook of the food provided by Jesus included 5000 *men*—to say nothing of women and children (Matthew 14:21). It would not be too much to assume that Jesus had the responsibility for feeding some 10,000 people in total. Using a small boy's lunch, which one of the disciples located, Jesus multiplied the meager serving of unleavened barley cakes and pickled fish until everyone in the vast crowd was more than satisfied. And there were 12 baskets of leftovers (John 6:1-15)!

Later that evening, Jesus dismissed the disciples and sent them back to Capernaum by boat across the northwest corner of the Sea of Galilee. On the Sea of Galilee, as the air cools in the evening, the winds typically pour down from the western heights to the surface of the lake, which is some 600 feet below sea level—and the result is a rough sea, rolling from west to east. This can often hinder progress for those traveling by boat.

In such a situation, the disciples found themselves working hard to advance in their homeward voyage but were making little if any progress. As they rowed with their backs to the wind, they suddenly noticed a human figure approaching them across the lake—*walking on the water.* As the figure gained on them, they became terrified and cried out in fear, thinking they were being pursued by a ghost. When Jesus approached them, He said, "It is I; don't be afraid" (John 6:20). After witnessing this miracle—and Jesus' accompanying miracle of enabling Peter to walk on water momentarily—the disciples worshiped Jesus in the boat, saying, "Truly you are the Son of God" (Matthew 14:33).

Turning water into wine, multiplying food to feed thousands, walking on water—these are not things mere mortals can do! They are clear "fingerprints" (or "signs") of a divine being, and that being is Jesus of Nazareth.

2. Jesus Healed People of Bodily Afflictions

Just as Jesus could sovereignly control the realm of nature as its Creator, so He could heal human bodies for the same reason. Jesus' ministry of healing sick people is a direct fulfillment of messianic prophecies in the Old Testament. One of these, Isaiah 35:5,6, predicted that when the Messiah came, "then will the eyes of the blind be opened and the ears of the deaf unstopped. Then will the lame leap like a deer, and the mute tongue shout for joy."

A representative example of such a miracle involves a royal official who came to Jesus and informed Him that his son was sick in Capernaum. The official begged Jesus to come and heal the lad—who at the time was near death. Jesus immediately granted the request and uttered a single, authoritative pronouncement: "You may go. Your son will live" (John 4:50).

Of course, this was a great test of faith for the royal official. By declaring that the boy was well again, Christ demanded that the official believe His word *without a single visible sign,* and *without the personal presence of the Savior at the boy's side.* What must have gone through the official's mind? Was not Jesus' word as good as His presence? Was He not able to perform all He promised? Our text indicates that the official "believed the word that Jesus spoke to him" (John 4:50 NASB). And the official would soon discover that his son was healed at the *precise time* Jesus had granted his request (verses 51-53). Such miracles constituted clear proof that Jesus was the promised divine Messiah!

3. Jesus Raised People from the Dead

Based on their understanding of the Old Testament Scriptures, the Jews believed that God is the only source of life. At the Creation, "the LORD God formed the man from the dust of the ground and breathed into his nostrils the breath of life, and the man became a living being" (Genesis 2:7). First Samuel 2:6 affirms that "the LORD brings death and makes alive; he brings down to the grave and raises up." And recall that the Egyptian magicians replicated the miraculous deeds of Moses *until* Moses was used by God to turn dust into living gnats, at which miracle they exclaimed, "This is the finger of God" (Exodus 8:19). This is why Jesus sent shock waves through the first-century Jewish community when He raised people from the dead. This is something only God could have done.

Jesus' power to restore life is vividly illustrated in Lazarus of Bethany. Jesus had been informed that His friend Lazarus was seriously ill, but He told the disciples that "this sickness will not end in death. No, it is for God's glory so that God's Son may be glorified through it" (John 11:4). Later, after purposefully delaying His visit to Lazarus, He omnisciently informed the disciples that Lazarus had died. But as He had promised, Jesus was glorified in what transpired, for at His command, Lazarus was raised from the dead—thereby attesting to the veracity of His words to Martha: "I am the resurrection and the life. He who believes in me will live, even though he dies; and whoever lives and believes in me will never die" (verses 25,26).

As noted previously, Jesus' miracles were recorded so that people may believe that He is the promised Messiah (John 20:30). In each miracle Jesus performed—whether it involved controlling the realm of nature, healing people of physical afflictions, or raising people from the dead—He distinguished Himself from weak and mortal man and attested to His true identity as Messiah-God. And many people have indeed ended up believing in Jesus as a result of these miracles.

But What About...?

Invariably, when I deal with the issue of Jesus' miracles in the New Testament, someone points to a particular verse in one of the Gospels and says, "But what about this verse that says...?"[2] Following are explanations of the more common "problem passages":

Why couldn't Jesus do miracles in His own hometown (Mark 6:4,5)?

In Mark 6:4,5 Jesus affirmed that a prophet is without honor in his hometown, and in view of that reality He could not perform any miracles in Nazareth except for healing a few sick people. The people of Nazareth were apparently plagued by unbelief and paid little attention to His claims.

At first glance, one might get the impression that Jesus' miraculous power was utterly dependent upon peoples' faith in order for it to work. That is not the meaning of this passage, however. It is not that Jesus was unable to perform or incapacitated in performing a miracle in Nazareth. Rather, Jesus "could not" do miracles there in the sense that He *would not* do so because of the pervasive unbelief in that city.

Miracles serve a far greater purpose from the divine perspective than just providing a raw display of power. Indeed, as noted previously, Jesus' miraculous deeds are called "signs" in the New Testament because they serve to *signify* His identity as the Messiah. Since the people of Nazareth had already made up their minds *against* Jesus and had provided more than ample evidence of their lack of faith in Him, Jesus chose not to engage in miraculous acts there except for healing a few of the sick. He refused to bestow miraculous *deeds* on a city that had rejected the miraculous *Messiah*. "Unbelief excluded the people of Nazareth from the dynamic disclosure of God's grace that others had experienced."[3]

Because of Nazareth's rejection of the person and message of Jesus Christ, He went on to other cities that *did* respond to and receive Him. There is no evidence Jesus ever again returned to Nazareth.

When Jesus said, "Someone touched me; I know that power has gone out from me" (Luke 8:46), did His intrinsic divine power cause a miracle without His purposing it?

In this verse we read that a woman who had been subject to bleeding for 12 years touched Jesus' garment and was instantly healed. Jesus then said, "Someone touched me; I know that power has gone out from me" (Luke 8:46). At first glance, it might seem Jesus was unaware of the identity of the woman. It might also appear that divine healing energy, without Jesus even intending or purposing it, was drawn out of His body and healed the woman. This is not the case, however.

Scripture portrays Jesus as *always* being in complete control of His divine miraculous power (see John 2:1-11; 4:50-52; 5:8,9; 11:40-44). People could not just walk up to Jesus, touch Him, and activate His miracle-working power *without His consent.* The reason the woman was healed when she touched Jesus' garment was that He *willed* her to be healed as a result of her *faith.*

The context indicates Jesus wanted this woman to "go public" with her faith that had led to her healing. Her desire to approach Jesus in stealth is understandable, since her hemorrhage rendered her ceremonially unclean (Leviticus 15:25-30). In addition to this, anyone who came into contact with her was also rendered unclean, according to the Jews. But Jesus forced her to "go public," as it were, and acknowledge it was she who touched Him.

Jesus wanted the woman to understand it was actually her *faith* that led to her healing (Luke 8:48). Jesus' cloak had no mysterious magical properties, but her touching of that cloak was an *expression* of her faith, which subsequently moved Jesus to heal her with His divine power. The woman's faith did indeed "go public" when she fell at Jesus' feet (verse 47).

There may be another reason Jesus wanted the woman to "go public." She was probably known in the community for her infirmity and was thus widely known as being unclean. By drawing attention to her healing, Jesus was publicly revealing to all present that she was no longer unclean and was fully healed.[4] She would thus be accepted back into society without hindrance.

Why did Jesus curse the fig tree and miraculously cause it to wither (Matthew 21:19)?

In Matthew 21 we find that Jesus was hungry and saw a fig tree by the side of the road. As He came close to it, He saw that it had no figs on it, so He cursed it and miraculously caused it to wither (verse 19). It may appear Jesus was just responding in anger to the tree, cursing it in tantrum-like behavior. But this is not the case. One must keep in mind the broader backdrop of Jesus' teaching methodology, which often involved parables and word pictures. Scholars agree that Jesus in the present case was performing a living parable—an *acted-out* parable—to teach His disciples an important truth. His cursing of the fig tree was a dramatic visual aid.

What important truth does the parable illustrate? Scholars have different opinions. Some say Jesus was illustrating the principle of faith to the disciples. If the disciples had such faith, they too could do such miracles as withering fig trees and moving mountains (see Matthew 17:20). They would need such faith in the hard days to come.

Other scholars believe that since the fig tree had leaves on it (Matthew 21:19), from a distance it gave the *appearance* of being fruitful. But upon closer examination it became clear there was no fruit on it at all. So perhaps Jesus' cursing of the fig tree was an acted-out parable that taught the disciples God will judge those who give an outer appearance of fruitfulness but in fact are not fruitful at all (like the Pharisees).

Still other scholars suggest the fig tree is representative of faithless Israel. Israel professed to be faithful to God and fruitful as a nation, but in fact she was *faithless* and *fruitless*. Indeed, Israel had rejected Jesus the Messiah and was thus ripe for judgment. Perhaps the withering of the fig tree foreshadowed the withering (or destruction) of Israel in A.D. 70 when Titus and his Roman warriors trampled on and destroyed Jerusalem, ending Israel as a political entity (see Luke 21:20).

And still other scholars see significance in the fact that the account of Jesus' cleansing of the temple in Mark's Gospel (Mark 11:15-19) is sandwiched between the two sections of Scripture dealing with the fig tree (verses 12-14 and 20-25). It is suggested that perhaps Jesus was teaching that at a distance the temple and its sacrificial activities looked fine. But on closer inspection it was found to be mere religion without substance, full of hypocrisy, bearing no spiritual fruit, ripe for judgment.

My opinion? I think the second option above—God judges those who *appear* fruitful but are not truly fruitful—has the most going for it. This was *truly* a miracle with a message.

Why did Jesus say the dead child was not dead but just asleep (Luke 8:51,52; Mark 5:39)?

Jairus had come to fetch Jesus in hopes of Him healing his daughter, who was on her deathbed. By the time they arrived at Jairus's house, they were informed that indeed the young girl had died. People at the house were wailing and mourning for her. Jesus then said, "Stop wailing....She is not dead but asleep" (Luke 8:51,52).

Why did Jesus say this? We know that the girl was physically dead, because verse 55 tells us that after Jesus healed her, her "spirit returned." (Death involves the departure of the soul or spirit from the body.)

Actually, this situation is not too difficult to explain. Jesus was simply saying that the girl's *present condition* of death was only temporary. He used the term "sleep" to indicate her condition was not permanent. He may have been saying that when *He* is involved in the picture, death really is as sleep, for it is temporary. As effortlessly as a parent awakens a child from sleep, so Jesus miraculously awakened the young girl from her temporary state of death (compare with John 11:11-14). We might paraphrase Jesus' words this way: "The girl is not permanently dead but only temporarily so. She is, metaphorically speaking, just asleep—and is soon to be supernaturally awakened in life."

Were all the sicknesses Jesus miraculously healed caused by demonic spirits (Matthew 12:22)?

In Matthew 12:22 we read: "Then they brought him a demon-possessed man who was blind and mute, and Jesus healed him, so that he could both talk and see." It might seem from verses such as this that perhaps all the sicknesses Jesus miraculously healed were caused by demonic spirits. But this is not the case.

On the one hand, it is true that Scripture portrays Satan and demons as inflicting physical diseases on people (such as *dumbness,* Matthew 9:33; *blindness,* 12:22; and *epilepsy,* 17:15-18). They can also afflict people with mental disorders (Mark 5:4,5; 9:22; Luke 8:27-29; 9:37-42) and can cause people to be self-destructive (Mark 5:5; Luke 9:42).

However, though demons can cause physical illnesses, Scripture distinguishes natural illnesses from demon-caused illnesses (Matthew 4:24; Mark 1:32; Luke 7:21; 9:1; Acts 5:16). In the case of numerous miraculous healings, no mention is made of demons. For example, no mention is made of demon affliction in the cases where Jesus healed the centurion's servant (Matthew 8:5-13), the woman with the hemorrhage of 12 years' duration (9:19,20), the two blind men (9:27-30), the man with the withered hand (12:9-14), and those who touched the fringe of Jesus' garment (14:35,36).

What did Jesus mean when He said His wicked generation would only be given the "sign of Jonah" (Luke 11:29,30)?

Jesus stated that though His wicked generation asked for a sign (miracle), the only sign it would be given would be the sign of Jonah: "For as Jonah was a sign to the Ninevites, so also will the Son of Man be to this generation" (Luke 11:29,30). What was Jesus saying here?

As a backdrop, the Jewish Pharisees had witnessed first-hand that Jesus was acting and speaking from a position of authority. They wondered what His authority was for acting and speaking in the way He did. In the Old Testament Moses had performed miracles before Pharaoh as a sign that demonstrated His authority came from God. Elijah, too, performed mighty miracles to prove His authority came from God. *What about Jesus?* Could He provide a sign to show His authority came from God?

The sinfulness of the Pharisees quickly becomes evident. For one thing, Jesus had *already* performed many mighty miracles that constituted signs that pointed to His true identity. Recall that one Pharisee (Nicodemus) said to Him, "Rabbi, we know you are a teacher who has come from God. For no one could perform the miraculous signs you are doing if God were not with him" (John 3:2). Most of the Pharisees, however, were hardhearted, and in their spiritual blindness rejected Jesus.

Jesus responded to the Pharisees' request for a sign as an indication of wickedness. The real issue in Jesus' mind was obedience to the Word of God and the One whom God had sent. Jesus therefore informed them they would be given only the sign of Jonah.

Though scholars have made a number of suggestions as to what the sign of Jonah is, the context seems to point to the resurrection of Jesus Christ. Jonah had been in the great fish for three days (Jonah 1:17) before, as it were, coming to life again by being regurgitated out of its mouth. After his reappearance, he spoke his message of repentance, and the Ninevites quickly responded. The sign to be given to *Jesus'* generation would be the reappearance of the Son of Man on the third day after His death. And, as one scholar put it, "Christ's return from death was as great a proof of His ministry as Jonah's rescue was of his."[5]

In what way was Jesus' resurrection a sign? Among other things, Romans 1:4 indicates that by the resurrection Jesus was declared to be the Son of God. Moreover, Jesus' resurrection guarantees the approaching judgment of all humankind (Acts 17:31). Hence, repentance is in order, every bit as much as repentance was in order among the Ninevites of Jonah's day.

Why did Jesus instruct the miraculously healed leper not to tell anyone but instead to go to the priest to offer sacrifices (Mark 1:44)?

In Mark 1:44 Jesus instructed the miraculously healed leper, "See that you don't tell this to anyone. But go, show yourself to the priest and offer the sacrifices that Moses commanded for your cleansing, as a testimony to them." There are two issues we must deal with here: 1) Why did Jesus instruct the man not to tell anyone? and 2) Why did Jesus send him to the priest to offer sacrifices?

As to why Jesus instructed the man not to tell anyone, He very well may have said this because of the popular misunderstandings that were floating around during that time about the Messiah. There was a very high expectation that when the Messiah came, He would deliver the Jews from Roman domination. The people were expecting a political Messiah/deliverer. So, for news that He was the Messiah to circulate at this early point in His ministry would immediately excite people's preconceived images of what this Messiah figure was supposed to do. The Romans might very well have then marked Him as a rebel leader.[6]

Seeking to avoid an erroneous popular response to His words and deeds, Jesus told the leper to keep quiet about the miracle. He did not want anyone speaking prematurely of His actual identity until He had had sufficient opportunity to make the character of His mission clear to the masses. As time passed on in His ministry, Christ's real identity became increasingly clear to those who came into contact with Him.

As to why Jesus instructed the man to go to the priest to offer sacrifices, He probably had in mind the Old Testament ritual requirements. The backdrop is that among the Jews leprosy was viewed as one of the worst forms of uncleanness.[7] According to the Mosaic Law, anyone who had leprosy, or who was even *thought* to have it, was required to undergo a ritual of cleansing in order to be accepted back into society. If this man had remained in Galilee, walking around and telling everyone how Christ had healed him, he would have been quickly categorized as "unclean" by all the Jews in the city, and his witness would have thus been nullified.

Scholars have noted there may be yet another reason why Christ sent the cleansed leper to the priest. He was sent in order to be a *witness* or *testimony* (Luke 5:14). The fact is, there was no record of a cleansed leper in Jewish history since the curing of Miriam in Numbers 12:10-15. So a cleansed leper would be very big news among the Jews.

Once the cleansed man had presented evidence to the priest that he had indeed been miraculously healed by Jesus, the priest would be forced to investigate the claim, and the evidence would then be presented to the Jewish Sanhedrin for a final declaration on the matter. Thus by sending the man to the priest, Christ was in essence sending evidence to the highest recognized authority among the Jews that the miracle-working Messiah was in their midst.

Jesus the Divine Messiah

In view of all the above, we conclude that the miracles recorded in the Gospels portray Jesus Christ as the Lord God of this world. Indeed, in His miracles we see Him as Lord of nature, Lord over life, Lord over death, Lord over sickness, Lord over sin, and Lord over Satan. The miracles are clear and eloquent evidence that Jesus of Nazareth possessed powers that belong only to God, and therefore that He is God Himself.

Points to Ponder

- Jesus proved His identity as the *one and only* Christ (Messiah) by His incredible miracles (signs).

- Today many cult leaders claim to be "the Christ" or "the Messiah" for our age. But they perform no miraculous signs such as Jesus did.

- When anyone today makes such boastful claims, you can rest assured he or she is *not* "the Christ," not only because he or she has no "signs" to back up the claim, but also because Jesus warned us about false Christs (Matthew 24:4-6).

- Such individuals are an example of Satan, not God, at work.

~

SEVEN

Miracles of the
New Testament Apostles

Just as the prophets were God's representatives in Old Testament times, so the apostles were God's representatives in New Testament times. The apostles were totally unique. Indeed, according to Scripture, the apostles were the special recipients of God's self-revelation. They were aware God was providing revelation through them (1 Corinthians 2:13; 1 Thessalonians 2:13; 1 John 1:1-3). They recognized their divine authority (1 Corinthians 7:10; 11:23). They were specially hand-picked by the Lord or the Holy Spirit (Matthew 10:1-4; Acts 1:26). The book of Revelation indicates the biblical apostles will be accorded a special honor by having their names inscribed on the 12 foundations of the eternal city in heaven (Revelation 21:14).

Scripture indicates an apostle had to be an eyewitness to the resurrected Christ. When Paul was defending his apostleship in 1 Corinthians 9:1, he said, "Am I not an apostle? Have I not seen Jesus our Lord?" Later in the same book, Paul said that the resurrected Christ appeared to James, then to all of the apostles, and finally ("last of all") to Paul himself (1 Corinthians 15:7,8). Obviously, no one living today can claim to have seen the resurrected Christ, and hence there can be no apostles today—*not in the biblical sense.* Paul was "last."

According to the New Testament, the biblical apostles were all authenticated by miraculous signs. In 2 Corinthians 12:12 Paul affirmed, "The things that mark an apostle—signs, wonders and miracles—were done among you with great perseverance." Note that the phrase "*were done* among you" is in the passive voice. Paul thus disowns any credit for the supernatural signs that accompanied his ministry.[1] God was the true source of the miracles. The apostles were only the instruments through which these miracles were performed.

In Romans 15:18,19 Paul affirmed, "I will not venture to speak of anything except what *Christ has accomplished through me* in leading the Gentiles to obey God by what I have said and done—by the power of signs and miracles, *through the power of the Spirit*" (emphasis added). Again, though the miracles were performed *through* Paul, he acknowledges it was God who was the true source.

In Acts 2:43 we read that "everyone was filled with awe, and many wonders and miraculous signs were done by [literally, *through*] the apostles" (insert added, see also Acts 5:12). It seems clear from such verses that the mark of a true apostle of God was the *God-sourced* ability to perform signs, wonders, and miracles. (See Chapter 3 for a discussion on the meaning of these terms.)

The apostle Peter, for example, healed a number of people (Acts 3:16; 9:32-35) and raised a person from the dead (9:36-42). The apostle Paul also raised a person from the dead (20:6-12). These and other works performed by the apostles constitute "signs, wonders and miracles" and distinguish the apostles from all pretended representatives of God. These miracles served to validate both the apostles *and* their message.

Notable Apostolic Miracles

Lame man is cured . . . . Acts 3:6
Instant death sentence against
    Ananias and Sapphira. . . . . Acts 5:5,10
Sick people healed . . . . Acts 5:15
Aeneas healed of paralysis . . . . Acts 9:34
Dorcas resurrected . . . . Acts 9:40
Lame man cured. . . . . Acts 14:10
Girl freed of evil spirits . . . . Acts 16:18
Eutychus resurrected . . . . Acts 20:10
Paul unharmed by snake bite. . . . . Acts 28:5
Publius's father healed . . . . Acts 28:8

Peter's resurrection of a female disciple named Tabitha (Dorcas) is especially noteworthy. I love this story from the book of Acts:

> In Joppa there was a disciple named Tabitha (which, when translated, is Dorcas), who was always doing good and helping the poor. About that time she became sick and died, and her body was washed and placed in an upstairs room. Lydda was near Joppa; so when the disciples heard that Peter was in Lydda, they sent two men to him and urged him, "Please come at once!"
>
> Peter went with them, and when he arrived he was taken upstairs to the room. All the widows stood around him, crying and showing him the robes and other clothing that Dorcas had made while she was still with them.
>
> Peter sent them all out of the room; then he got down on his knees and prayed. Turning toward the dead woman, he said, "Tabitha, get up." She opened her eyes, and seeing Peter she sat up. He took her by the hand and helped her to her feet. Then he called the believers and the widows and presented her to

them alive. This became known all over Joppa, and many people believed in the Lord (Acts 9:36-42).

Pay special attention to this last verse: "This became known all over Joppa, and many people believed in the Lord" (Acts 9:42). Like the other miracles, this one was a tremendous testimony of the one true God, and many placed their faith in the Lord Jesus as a result of it. Peter was not the "star of the show," but rather the Lord was. The people placed their faith *in the Lord*, not Peter. The miracle exalted *the Lord*, not Peter.

Another tremendous miracle performed by the apostle Peter is recorded for us in Acts 3:2-10 (pay special attention to the italicized words):

> Now a man crippled from birth was being carried to the temple gate called Beautiful, where he was put every day to beg from those going into the temple courts. When he saw Peter and John about to enter, he asked them for money. Peter looked straight at him, as did John. Then Peter said, "Look at us!" So the man gave them his attention, expecting to get something from them.
>
> Then Peter said, "Silver or gold I do not have, but what I have I give you. *In the name of Jesus Christ of Nazareth*, walk." Taking him by the right hand, he helped him up, and instantly the man's feet and ankles became strong. He jumped to his feet and began to walk. Then he went with them into the temple courts, walking and jumping, and *praising God.* When all the people saw him walking and *praising God*, they recognized him as the same man who used to sit begging at the temple gate called Beautiful, and they were filled with wonder and amazement at what had happened to him.

One thing that becomes abundantly clear as we study the miracles of the apostles is that they never claimed to do such miracles in their own power but rather in the power of God Himself. I want to draw your attention to the fact that in Acts 3:12 the apostle Peter said to the people who had just witnessed the miracle recounted above: "Why do you stare at us as if by our own power or godliness we had made this man walk?" Peter pointed to the fact that *it was God* who did this miracle through the apostles. The backdrop relates to the Upper Room discourse where Jesus had informed the apostles, "Apart from me you can do nothing" (John 15:5). God is always portrayed as the only true source of miracles.

This is an *extremely* important point, because there were many in ancient cultures who misunderstood the true source of miracles. A good example of this relates to the miracle the apostle Paul performed in Lystra:

> In Lystra there sat a man crippled in his feet, who was lame from birth and had never walked. He listened to Paul as he was speaking. Paul looked directly at him, saw that he had faith to be healed and called out, "Stand up on your feet!" At that, the man jumped up and began to walk.
>
> When the crowd saw what Paul had done, they shouted in the Lycaonian language, "The gods have come down to us in human form!" Barnabas they called Zeus, and Paul they called Hermes because he was the chief speaker. The priest of Zeus, whose temple was just outside the city, brought bulls and wreaths to the city gates because he and the crowd wanted to offer sacrifices to them.
>
> But when the apostles Barnabas and Paul heard of this, they tore their clothes and rushed out into the crowd, shouting: "Men, why are you doing this? We too are only men, human like you. We are bringing you good news, telling you to turn from these worthless things to the living God, who made heaven and earth and sea and everything in them. In the past, he

> let all nations go their own way. Yet he has not left
> himself without testimony: He has shown kindness by
> giving you rain from heaven and crops in their sea-
> sons; he provides you with plenty of food and fills
> your hearts with joy." Even with these words, they had
> difficulty keeping the crowd from sacrificing to them
> (Acts 14:8-18).

The backdrop to this passage is that pagan cultures were polytheistic—that is, they believed in *many* gods who were thought to perform a variety of functions. Pagans thought that some "gods" could produce abundant crops; others were thought to affect the weather; still others were thought to heal people, and so on. When Paul miraculously healed the crippled man, this pagan group thought they had such a god in their midst.

As soon as the crowd witnessed the mighty miracle, they said "the gods are come down to us in the likeness of men" (Acts 14:11). This must be understood against the backdrop of a local legend. The story is told of an elderly, pious couple—Philemon and Baucis—who, without realizing it, entertained two gods: Jupiter and Mercury (the Roman equivalents of Zeus and Hermes). These gods were said to have generously rewarded the couple for their hospitality.

According to the legend, the gods had taken human form and had sought lodging at a thousand different houses, but Philemon and Baucis were the only ones who took them in. The gods reciprocated by transforming their humble cottage of straw and reeds into a temple with a golden roof.[2] The people of Lystra were therefore watchful and expectant as they awaited another visitation of the gods in their community.

After witnessing the miracle, the people excitedly called Barnabas "Zeus," and Paul "Hermes" (Acts 14:12). New Testament scholar F. F. Bruce tells us that

Zeus was the chief god in the Greek Pantheon; Hermes, son of Zeus by Maia, was the herald of the gods. Barnabas may have been identified with Zeus because of his more dignified bearing; Paul, the more animated of the two, was called Hermes "because he was the chief speaker."[3]

Because the people in the crowd spoke in their native language (Lycaonian), it is likely that Paul and Barnabas could not understand what they were saying. It wasn't until the people began preparing to offer sacrifices to them that they caught on to what was really happening.

As soon as Paul and Barnabas knew what was going on, they tore their clothing. This was an expression of horror—a way of showing strong aversion to blasphemy. Usually such rips were made four or five inches into the neckline of the garment.[4] By engaging in this action, Paul and Barnabas were demonstrating in a graphic way that what the people had done was absolutely unacceptable and forbidden before the one true God.

Paul immediately began preaching, and he emphasized that he and Barnabas were men, just like them. Moreover, Paul said, the *true* God—the Creator of the universe—has not left Himself without a witness (Acts 14:17): His works of creating and sustaining the universe show Him to be a caring and benevolent God.

Despite Paul's words about the one true God, he and Barnabas still had a difficult time keeping the crowd from offering sacrifices to them. So powerful was this miracle—so awesome and so wondrous—that the people knew something supernatural had occurred. But because of their pagan background, they completely misread the situation.

In any event, Paul, like Peter, knew the importance of emphasizing that the apostles were mere instruments of God. They did not perform miracles in their own power but rather did them in the power of the one true miracle-working God.

Paul, like Peter, pointed the attention away from himself and toward God.

I believe there is an important lesson for us here. The sad reality is that some of today's most popular televangelists seem to always be pointing the attention not to God but to themselves. They engage in all kinds of glittery theatrics on television that make people go "ooh" and "ah." They make such a show of it—and they are raking in huge financial profits in the process. When you see such things on television in the future, I hope "red flags" will immediately be raised in your mind as to whether these individuals are truly acting on God's behalf.

Handkerchief Miracles Today?

According to Acts 19:12, even handkerchiefs and aprons that had touched the apostle Paul "were taken to the sick, and their illnesses were cured and the evil spirits left them." Based on this verse, some modern ministries have distributed "miracle prayer clothes" and various other items in exchange for a nice donation to the ministry. This is a complete abuse of this Scripture verse.

In the first place, *only the apostles* were given the special signs of an apostle (2 Corinthians 12:12). The apostles were the unique representatives of God, and once the apostles passed off the scene, their unique sign gifts passed with them (see Hebrews 2:3,4). These special signs served to confirm God's special revelation through them (revelation that was later inscripturated—made into Scripture—in the pages of the New Testament).

In the second place, Acts 19:12 is *descriptive*, not *prescriptive*. In other words, this passage *describes* a unique event that took place in relation to an apostle of God. It does not *prescribe* something that would be repeated throughout church history.

Interestingly, some Roman Catholics cite this verse in support of their doctrine of the veneration of relics. However, nowhere does it say here or anywhere else in the New Testament that articles through which miracles were performed were to be venerated. It is noteworthy that God not only forbade such idolatry in general in the Old Testament (Exodus 20:4,5), but when any object (such as the brazen serpent) that was used by God for a miracle was venerated, it was considered idolatry (see 2 Kings 18:4). Christians should *always* steer clear of this type of thing.

Have Apostolic Miracles Ceased?

Many scholars have pointed out that, inasmuch as there are no longer apostles today, then apostolic miracles have ceased as well. In Hebrews 2:3,4 we read: "This salvation, which was first announced by the Lord, *was confirmed to us by those who heard him.* God also testified to it by signs, wonders and various miracles, and gifts of the Holy Spirit distributed according to his will" (emphasis added). The book of Hebrews was written somewhere between A.D. 64 and 68, so apparently by this time God's work of "confirming" His message was nearing an end, and the apostolic miracles were waning. Late in his apostolic work, the apostle Paul was apparently unable to heal Epaphroditus (Philippians 2:25-27), Trophimus (2 Timothy 4:20), and Timothy (1 Timothy 5:23). Earlier Paul had not only healed people (Acts 14:8-18), but had raised people from the dead (Acts 20:6-12).

We are also told in Ephesians 2:20 that the church is "built on the foundation of the apostles and prophets, with Christ Jesus himself as the chief cornerstone." Once a foundation is built, it does not need to be built *again* but is rather built *upon*. Apostleship is by its very nature a foundational gift. And because it is foundational, it is not something that continues throughout each succeeding generation.

Yet, to say that apostolic miracles have ceased *is not* to say God has ceased *all* miracles, or that God has ceased working providentially among His people with mighty answers to prayer. God still does miraculous things when He so chooses—but He does so much less often than in apostolic times.

Points to Ponder

- Apostles in the biblical sense were attested to by the "signs" of an apostle—miraculous signs and wonders (2 Corinthians 12:12).

- Miracles thus served to distinguish *true* apostles from pretended representatives of God.

- Today, many claim to be apostles of God, setting forth new revelations from God. You may be certain that these are not true *biblical* apostles, for they do not display the "signs" of an apostle (miraculous signs and wonders).

- Note also that the biblical apostles always gave credit to and glorified God *alone* in all miracles (Romans 15:18,19).

- If you witness a so-called apostle of God that puts on a show and exalts himself in connection with alleged miraculous phenomena, you may assume this is not of God.

~

EIGHT

The New Testament Miracle of Miracles: The Resurrection

Dwight L. Moody, one of the great evangelists of the nineteenth century, reminded us: "You can't find directions in the New Testament on how to conduct a funeral because Jesus broke up every funeral He attended."[1] Not only did Jesus break up every funeral He attended by resurrecting the dead, He also broke up *His own* funeral by rising from the dead *Himself* (John 2:19)! Truly the resurrection is a mammoth miracle in a league of its own. Understandably, this single miracle is foundational to the very survival and truth of Christianity. As one scholar put it:

> It should be clear...that the central miracle of NT [New Testament] religion is the resurrection of Christ. Without this miracle the early church would not have come into being, and we who live in the twentieth century would no doubt never have heard of the other NT miracles. Indeed, we would probably never have heard of Jesus of Nazareth, who would have been forgotten along with hundreds of other

obscure preachers and miracle workers who wandered about the ancient Middle East.[2]

Theologian Henry Clarence Thiessen is correct when he says "if the resurrection of Christ is a historical fact, then the way is opened for the acceptance of the other miracles also."[3] As we will see in what follows, the resurrection of Christ from the dead is one of the best-attested historical events of ancient history.

Allegations of the Critics

Both friends and enemies of Christianity have long recognized that the resurrection of Christ is the foundation stone of the Christian faith. The apostle Paul wrote to the Corinthians: "If Christ has not been raised, your faith is futile; you are still in your sins" (1 Corinthians 15:17).

Paul realized that the most important truths of Christianity stand or fall on the doctrine of Christ's resurrection. If Christ did not rise from the dead, then Christianity is little more than an interesting museum piece.

Certainly there have been those in every century who have tried to challenge the doctrine of the resurrection. One of the modern challenges comes from a self-appointed group of liberal scholars who call themselves "The Jesus Seminar." In a *Time* magazine article entitled "The Message of Miracles: Religious Controversy Over Validity of Miracles," we read: "Dominique Crossan, who is cochairman of the seminar...argues it this way: since the Crucifixion was conducted by Roman soldiers, Jesus' body was most likely left on the Cross or tossed into a shallow grave to be eaten by scavenger dogs, crows or other wild beasts."[4] So—Jesus wasn't resurrected: He was just eaten by dogs, and that was the end of that. Crossan, of course, offers no proof for this assertion, for there is none. A look at the hard evidence points to the genuine reality of the resurrection.

The Crucifixion and Burial of Jesus Christ

Following His crucifixion, the body of Jesus was buried in accordance with Jewish burial customs. He was wrapped in a linen cloth. Then about 100 pounds of aromatic spices—mixed together to form a gummy substance—were applied to the wrappings of cloth around His body.

After His body was placed in a tomb hewn out of solid rock, an extremely large stone was rolled against the entrance with levers. This stone would have weighed somewhere around two tons (4000 pounds). It is not a stone that would have been easily moved by human beings.

Roman guards were then stationed at the tomb. These strictly disciplined men were highly motivated to succeed in all they were assigned by the Roman government. Fear of cruel punishment produced flawless attention to duty, especially in the night watches. These Roman guards would have affixed on the tomb the Roman seal, a stamp representing Roman power and authority.

All this makes the situation at the tomb following Christ's resurrection highly significant. The Roman seal was broken, which meant, without exception, crucifixion upside-down for the person responsible. Furthermore, the large stone was moved a good distance from the entrance, as if it had been picked up and carried away. The Roman guards had also fled. The penalty in Rome for a guard leaving his position was death. We can therefore assume they must have had a substantial reason for fleeing!

The Evidence for Christ's Resurrection

The biblical testimony tells us Jesus first attested to His resurrection by appearing to Mary Magdalene (John 20:10-18)—a fact which, to me, is a highly significant indicator of the authenticity and reliability of the resurrection account. If the resurrection story were a fabrication, made up by the disciples, *no one in the first-century Jewish culture would have invented it this way.* The fact is that in Jewish law a woman's testimony was unacceptable in any court of law except in a very few circumstances. A fabricator would have been much more likely to represent Peter or the other male disciples as the first people at the tomb. But our biblical text tells us the Lord appeared first to Mary because *that was the way it actually happened.*

Following this, Mary promptly told the disciples the glorious news. That evening, the disciples had gathered in a room with the doors shut for fear of the Jews (John 20:19). This fear was well founded, for after Jesus had been arrested, Annas the high priest specifically asked Jesus about the disciples (18:19). Jesus had also previously warned the disciples in the upper room: "If they persecuted me, they will persecute you also" (15:20). These facts no doubt lingered in their minds after Jesus was brutally crucified.

But then their gloom turned to joy. The risen Christ appeared in their midst and said to them, "Peace be with you" (John 20:19). This phrase was a common Hebrew greeting (1 Samuel 25:6). But on this occasion there was added significance to Jesus' words. After their conduct on Good Friday (they had all scattered like a bunch of spineless cowards after Jesus' arrest), the disciples may well have expected a rebuke from Jesus. Instead, He displayed compassion by pronouncing peace upon them.

Jesus immediately showed the disciples His hands and His side (John 20:20). The risen Lord wanted them to see it was truly He. The wounds showed He did not have another body but the *same* body. He was dead, but now He is alive forevermore.

Now, consider this: By all accounts, the disciples came away from the crucifixion frightened and full of doubt. And yet, following Jesus' resurrection appearance to the disciples, their lives were virtually transformed. *The cowards became bulwarks of courage, fearless defenders of the faith.* The only thing that could account for this incredible transformation was the resurrection.

As the days passed, Jesus continued to make many appearances and proved He had indeed truly risen from the dead. Acts 1:3 says, "He showed himself to these men and gave many convincing proofs that he was alive. He appeared to them over a period of forty days and spoke about the kingdom of God." Moreover, "He appeared to more than five hundred of the brothers at the same time, most of whom are still living, though some have fallen asleep" (1 Corinthians 15:6). It seems clear that the resurrection of Christ is one of the best-attested historical events of ancient times.

The Resurrection Was an Actual, Physical Event

There have been many who have tried to lessen the impact of the resurrection of Christ by arguing that it was a nonphysical event. *Time* magazine reports one of these theories:

> "[The Gospels] were talking not about the resurrection of the flesh but about the resurrection of Christ's selfhood, his essence," says Jackson Carroll, a professor of religion and society at Duke Divinity School. "The authors of the New Testament had experiences with an extraordinary person and extraordinary events, and they were trying to find ways to talk about all that. They weren't writing scientific history; they were writing faith history."[5]

This seems a rather preposterous interpretation. It amounts to saying that the disciples—all raised in Judaism with high respect for the Ten Commandments (which

instruct people not to lie and not to bear false witness)—
conspired together in a fantastic lie, which they all chose to
defend by laying down their very lives. The New Testament
witnesses not only laid down their lives, they also suffered
greatly during their lifetimes for their beliefs—something
that is unimaginable unless that which they were defending
was true.

In 2 Corinthians 4:8,9 we read of Paul and the apostles:
"We are hard pressed on every side, but not crushed; perplexed, but not in despair; persecuted, but not abandoned;
struck down, but not destroyed." This doesn't sound like
very much fun to endure for the sake of a lie!

We also read of Paul:

> Five times I received from the Jews the forty lashes
> minus one. Three times I was beaten with rods, once
> I was stoned, three times I was shipwrecked, I spent a
> night and a day in the open sea, I have been con-
> stantly on the move. I have been in danger from
> rivers, in danger from bandits, in danger from my
> own countrymen, in danger from Gentiles; in danger
> in the city, in danger in the country, in danger at sea;
> and in danger from false brothers. I have labored and
> toiled and have often gone without sleep; I have
> known hunger and thirst and have often gone
> without food; I have been cold and naked (2 Corin-
> thians 11:24-27).

So—the liberal scholars expect us to believe that not only
did the apostles suffer incredibly during their lives but also
ended up laying down their lives, *all for the sake of an elaborate
lie?* I think it takes more faith to believe *that* theory than it
does to believe the actual account of the resurrection.

Another point that bears consideration is if Jesus' followers concocted events like the resurrection, wouldn't
Jesus' critics have then immediately come forward to
debunk these lies and put an end to Christianity once and

for all? It is worth noting that the apostle Paul in 1 Corinthians 15:1-4 speaks of Christ's resurrection as part of a public confession that had been handed down for years. First Corinthians was written around A.D. 55, a mere 20 years after Christ's resurrection. But biblical scholars believe the confession in 1 Corinthians 15:1-4 was formulated within just a few years of Jesus' death and resurrection. As noted previously, Paul said the resurrected Christ appeared to more than 500 people at a single time, "most of whom are still living" (1 Corinthians 15:6). If Paul had misrepresented the facts, wouldn't one of these 500 have come forward to dispute his claims? But no one came forward to dispute anything—because *the resurrection really occurred.*

As for the *physical* nature of the resurrection (as opposed to Jesus' "selfhood" or "essence" being "resurrected"—whatever *that* means!), I begin with the observation that the Greek word for "body" *(soma),* when used of a person, always means *physical* body in the New Testament. There are no exceptions to this. Greek scholar Robert Gundry, in his authoritative book *Soma in Biblical Theology* (published by Cambridge University Press), speaks of "Paul's exceptionless use of *soma* for a physical body."[6] Hence, all references to Jesus' resurrection "body" *(soma)* in the New Testament must be taken to mean a resurrected *physical* body.

In further support of the physical nature of Christ's resurrection is the fact Christ Himself said to the disciples: "See My hands and My feet, that it is I Myself; touch Me and see, for a spirit does not have flesh and bones as you see that I have" (Luke 24:39 NASB). Notice three things here: 1) The resurrected Christ indicates in this verse He is not a spirit; 2) The resurrected Christ indicates His resurrection body is made up of flesh and bones; and 3) Christ's physical hands and feet represent physical proof of the materiality of His resurrection from the dead.

Furthermore, consider the verbal exchange that took place between Jesus and some Jewish leaders recorded in

John 2:19-21: "Jesus answered them, 'Destroy this temple, and I will raise it again in three days.' The Jews replied, 'It has taken forty-six years to build this temple, and you are going to raise it in three days?' But the temple he had spoken of was his body." Jesus here said that He would be raised from the dead *bodily*.

We also note the resurrected Christ ate physical food on four different occasions. And He did this as a means of proving He had a real physical body (Luke 24:30; 24:42,43; John 21:12,13; Acts 1:4).

Still further, the physical body of the resurrected Christ was touched and handled by various people. For example, He was touched by Mary (John 20:17) and by some women (Matthew 28:9). He also challenged the disciples to physically touch Him so they could rest assured His body was material in nature (Luke 24:39).

Finally, we note the teaching of the apostle Paul that the body that is "sown" in death is the *very same* body that is raised in life (1 Corinthians 15:35-44). That which goes into the grave is raised to life (see verse 42).

Answering Foolish Theories About the Resurrection

It is beyond the scope of this chapter to answer all of the foolish theories that have emerged through the years by unbelievers trying to explain away the resurrection of Christ. But I want to mention at least three of the more prominent ones.

The "Passover Plot" Theory

Some years ago, a Jewish scholar by the name of Hugh Schonfield developed a theory and wrote a book on it called *The Passover Plot*. Schonfield argued that Jesus conspired with

Joseph of Arimathea, Lazarus, and an anonymous young man to convince His disciples He was the Messiah. He allegedly manipulated events to make it appear He was the fulfillment of numerous prophecies. Regarding the resurrection, Jesus allegedly took some drugs and feigned death but was revived later. Unfortunately, the crucifixion wounds ultimately proved fatal, and He died. The plotters then stole and disposed of Jesus' body, and the appearances of Christ were simply a case of mistaken identity.

This theory is full of holes. First, Christ was of the highest moral character in the way He lived His life and in His teachings. It goes beyond all credibility to say Jesus was deceitful and sought to fool people into believing He was the Messiah. Moreover, there are many prophecies fulfilled in the person of Jesus that He couldn't have conspired to fulfill—such as His birth in Bethlehem (Micah 5:2), being born of a virgin (Isaiah 7:14), and the identity of His forerunner, John the Baptist (Malachi 3:1).

It is also highly unlikely that the plotters could have stolen Jesus' dead body in order to dispose of it. The tomb had a huge stone (weighing several tons) blocking it, had a seal of the Roman government, and was protected by strong Roman guards trained in the art of defense and killing.

The idea that the appearances of Christ were simply a case of mistaken identity is ridiculous. Jesus appeared to *too many people* (including 500 at a single time—1 Corinthians 15:6), on *too many occasions* (12), over *too long a time* (40 days), for this to be the case.

The Wrong Tomb Theory

There are some who have tried to explain away Christ's resurrection by saying the women and the disciples went to the wrong tomb—and when they didn't see the dead body of Jesus, they merely assumed He had risen from the dead. To believe in this theory, we would have to conclude that the *women* went to the wrong tomb, that *Peter and John* ran to the wrong tomb, that the *Jews* then went to the wrong tomb, followed by the *Jewish Sanhedrin* and *the Romans* who went to the wrong tomb. We'd have to say that *Joseph of Arimathea*, the owner of the tomb, also went to the wrong tomb. In addition, the *angel from heaven* must have appeared at the wrong tomb. Besides all this, how are the many postresurrection appearances of Christ to be explained—including the appearance to over 500 people at a single time (1 Corinthians 15:6)? This theory is grasping at straws in its attempt to deny the resurrection.

The Swoon Theory

This theory suggests Jesus didn't really die on the cross. He was nailed to the cross and suffered from loss of blood and went into shock. But He didn't die. He merely fainted (or *swooned*) from exhaustion. The disciples mistook Him for dead and buried Him alive in a tomb. They were easily fooled, living in the first century as they did. Suddenly, the cold atmosphere of the tomb woke Jesus from His state of shock. And when Jesus emerged from the tomb and was seen by the disciples, they knew He must have been raised from the dead.

This theory is highly imaginative. In fact, I think it is another one of those theories that requires more faith to believe than the actual resurrection account. Consider the facts and the claims of this theory:

- Jesus went through six trials and was beaten beyond description.

- He was so weak that He couldn't even carry the wooden cross bar.

- Huge spikes were driven through His wrists and feet.

- A Roman soldier thrust a spear into His side so that blood and water came out.

- Four Roman executioners (who had many years of experience in their line of work) goofed and mistakenly pronounced Jesus dead.

- Over a hundred pounds of gummy spices were applied to Jesus' body, and during this process, no one saw Jesus breathing.

- A large stone weighing several tons was rolled against the tomb; Roman guards were placed there; and a seal wrapped across the entrance.

- Jesus awoke in the cool tomb, split off the grave garments, pushed the several-ton stone away, fought off the Roman guards, and appeared to the disciples. *I don't think so.*

All the explanations that have been raised against the resurrection of Christ are simply futile denials of unbelievers whose hearts are hardened against God. The evidence for the resurrection is there for any to examine. It is a miracle of miracles with the stamp of historical authenticity.

Weighing the Evidence

The attack on Christianity by its enemies has most often concentrated on the resurrection of Christ, because it has been correctly seen that this event is the foundation of the Christian faith. An extraordinary attack was launched in the 1930s by a young British lawyer. He was convinced that the resurrection of Christ was sheer fantasy and fable. Perceiving that this doctrine was the keystone of the Christian faith, he decided to gather the available evidence and expose this fraud once and for all.

Since he was a lawyer, he was confident he had the necessary mental equipment to rigorously sift through all the evidence. He was determined not to admit anything into evidence that did not meet the same stiff criteria for admission that modern law courts demand.

While doing his research, however, a funny thing happened. He discovered that the case against Christ's resurrection was not nearly so airtight as he had presumed. As a result, the first chapter of his book ended up being entitled, "The Book that Refused to be Written." In it he describes how—after examining the indisputable evidence—he became persuaded against his will that Christ *really did* bodily rise from the dead. The book is called *Who Moved the Stone?* Its author is Frank Morison.

Morison made the same discovery countless others have made down through the centuries. He discovered that the factual evidence for Christ's resurrection is truly staggering. Canon Westcott, a brilliant scholar at Cambridge University, said it well: "Taking all the evidence together, it is not too much to say that there is no historic incident better or more variously supported than the resurrection of Christ."[7]

Sir Edward Clarke similarly said, "As a lawyer, I have made a prolonged study of the evidences for the events of the first Easter Day. To me, the evidence is conclusive, and over and over again in the High Court I have secured the verdict on evidence not nearly so compelling."[8]

Professor Thomas Arnold was the author of the famous three-volume *History of Rome* and was appointed to the Chair of Modern History at Oxford University. He was well-acquainted with the value of evidence in determining historical facts. After examining all the data on Christ's resurrection, he concluded: "I know of no one fact in the history of mankind which is proved by better and fuller evidence of every sort, to the understanding of a fair inquiry, than the great sign which God has given us that Christ died and rose again from the dead."[9]

The Resurrection Miracle Continued

At the beginning of this chapter I mentioned that if the resurrection of Christ is a historical fact, then the way is opened for the acceptance of the other miracles also. One of the "other miracles" I am referring to is the fact that we too shall one day be resurrected. *The miracle continues!* Jesus' historical resurrection from the dead paves the way for our miraculous future—a future in which we too will be resurrected and live forever with God in heaven.

Recall that following the death of Lazarus, Jesus told Lazarus's sister: "I am the resurrection and the life. He who believes in me will live, even though he dies; and whoever lives and believes in me will never die" (John 11:25,26). To prove His authority to make such statements, Jesus promptly raised Lazarus from the dead!

Jesus on another occasion affirmed, "This is the will of him who sent me, that I shall lose none of all that he has given me, but raise them up at the last day. For my Father's will is that everyone who looks to the Son and believes in him shall have eternal life, and I will raise him up at the last day" (John 6:39,40).

Hence, because of what Jesus Himself accomplished on our behalf, *we too* shall be resurrected from the dead. We can rest in the quiet assurance that even though our mortal bodies may pass away in death, they will be gloriously raised, never again to grow old and die. *We too shall experience the miracle of the resurrection!*

Points to Ponder

- The account of the resurrection in the Gospels illustrates the need for presenting hard evidence when a tremendous miracle occurs.

- Today, many miracle claims are being made that are virtually unsubstantiated.

- While miracles of God *can* occur, many claimed miracles today are false, with no evidence to support them.

- Insisting on evidence is not rooted in a lack of faith. It is rooted in a commitment to God's truth.

- Just as Jesus provided "convincing proofs" for the miracle of the resurrection (Acts 1:3), so we should seek convincing proofs regarding all miracle claims. And when a genuine miracle does happen, we can rejoice.

~

NINE

The Possibility of Miracles Today

I want to begin this chapter with an account of a modern miracle as told by Chuck Swindoll, as reliable a spokesman for God as there is in our modern era. Consider his words:

> Back in the late 1950s I became close friends with a man who had been a fellow Marine. Our friendship deepened as time passed, even though miles separated us. I was ministering in the state of Massachusetts, and he lived in Texas. Then one day I received a call from him.
>
> "I need your prayers as I've never needed them before," he said in a rather grim voice. My immediate response was: "What is it?"
>
> He said, "I have been diagnosed as having cancer of the tongue....The doctor says I have this malignant tumor. It is clearly evident in the X-rays. I just want you to pray that God, if it is His perfect will, will do a miracle." I assured him we would certainly pray with and for him.
>
> As soon as I hung up the phone, I walked down the stairs to a little place in our basement where I

would often go for quietness and prayer. Cynthia prayed with me for a while, then left to care for our children, who were still small. I stayed for almost an hour, and as I prayed, God's "unidentified inner prompting" gave me an unusual sense of reassurance. I did not hear any voice. I did not see any vision. But I had an unusual feeling of confidence and a sense of peace about my friend's situation. I read several Scriptures, prayed for perhaps 45 minutes, then left it with God.

Two or three days later my phone rang again. I heard the voice of my friend on the other end of the line. By then he was in Minnesota, calling me from the Mayo Clinic.

"I have great news," he said.

I smiled to myself. "Well, what is it?"

"I have seen several specialists, and my wife and I have just met with our attending physician. He is baffled, Chuck. He tells us there is no cancer."

"Hey, this is great!" I replied. "Tell me what they said."

"Well," he responded, "actually they put me through all the tests again and took more X-rays. They don't believe I brought the correct X-rays with me, because the X-rays they took disagree so much with the ones I brought. I now have before me two sets of X-rays. One shows the cancer in the tongue as it was in Dallas. The other X-rays, taken here in Minnesota, are clear—no cancer." And with a touch of humor he continued, "So we had a remarkable flight from Dallas to Minnesota. Somehow, in some miraculous manner, the malignant tumor is nowhere to be found."

It was not only miraculous, it was also instantaneous, and it remained permanent. He never again had a problem with the pain or the growth in his tongue. My friend was a middle-aged man and had many wonderful years in front of him, which he lived to the fullest. His subsequent death—many years later—was brought on by an unrelated disease.

I can't explain what happened. He couldn't either. I have no powers within me that produce healing in anyone else. The God I know is the same God you know, and I simply trusted Him and prayed for His will to be done. The Spirit of God healed my friend sovereignly and silently. And best of all, God got all the glory.[1]

I believe this is an account of a genuine miracle in modern times. Swindoll is not one who is given to sensationalism. He has been shown over and over again to be trustworthy and truthful. I've met the man, and I've always been impressed with his genuineness and integrity.

Do miracles happen today? I believe they do. But I must qualify what I mean by this. These are days for discernment. When we talk about the possibility of miracles today, we need to be careful because there is *so much* imbalanced thinking about this issue that is being disseminated through the popular media.

History Anyone?

I know many people who are bored with history. I've always been fascinated by history, because history is all about people and what people have done in the past. When it comes to the issue of miracles, there are some important things we can learn from history.

The primary point I want to make here is that when one examines biblical history, there seems to be perhaps four primary periods in which miracles are concentrated or clustered. These are the periods of:

1. *Moses and Joshua* (the ten plagues inflicted on Egypt, the crossing of the Red Sea, the provision of manna in the wilderness, and the collapse of the walls of Jericho);

2. *Elijah and Elisha* (the resurrection of a widow's son, curing leprosy, fire from heaven that consumed Elijah's sacrifice and destroyed the prophets of Baal, miraculous falling of rain, and the multiplication of 20 loaves of new barley into a supply sufficient for 100 men);

3. *Daniel* (God's miraculous preservation of Shadrach, Meshach, and Abednego in the fiery furnace, and God's preservation of Daniel in the lion's den); and

4. *Christ and the apostles* (mighty healings, casting out of demons, feeding 5000 people, walking on water, turning water into wine, calming storms, and resurrecting people from the dead—especially Christ's resurrection *of Himself* from the dead).

In between these periods, miracles still occurred. But they occurred *less frequently* than during these four concentrated periods. As C.S. Lewis put it, "God does not shake miracles into Nature at random as if from a pepper-caster. They come on great occasions: they are found at the great ganglions of history—not of political or social history, but of spiritual history which cannot be fully known by men."[2] It seems the miracles occurred most frequently during periods of God's *self-revelation* to humankind.[3] The miracles that occurred during these periods "were irrefutable signs from God that were designed to authenticate God's revealed Word (the law, the prophets, and the New Testament)."[4]

I make this point for a reason. If it is true that even in biblical times there was not one miracle after another in rapid succession, then certainly to a much greater extent Christians should not be expecting one miracle after another today.[5] Yes, great miracles *do* occur today (as in the case of Chuck Swindoll's friend), but they are occasional. Contrary to what some popular televangelists may say to their vast television audiences, the reality is that miracles do not occur today with the frequency of New Testament times when the apostles were alive and active.

Even as the apostles themselves were aging, it seems that the occurrence of miracles began to taper off with less intensity. There came a time when Paul could not heal Epaphroditus (Philippians 2:25-30) or Timothy (1 Timothy 5:23) or even himself (2 Corinthians 12:7-9). God's time of self-revelation was apparently coming to a close toward the end of the apostles' lives. Yes, God would still do miracles, but less frequently. Pastor Douglas Connelly notes: "The contrast is remarkable! At the beginning of the book of Acts, multitudes are being healed; at the end of New Testament history, the companions of the apostles have to be left behind because of serious illness."[6]

Miracles Today

As I began doing research for this chapter, I anticipated coming across numerous academic biblical scholars who would say miracles after New Testament times are an absolute impossibility. To be sure, there are some who *do* hold to that position. But I encountered many respectable theologians who argued otherwise.

- Church father Augustine believed in miracles during his time (fifth century), though he believed they were fewer and less public than those performed in New Testament times.[7] In fact, in his book *The City of God* (Book 22:8), he declared that over a span of less than two years he became aware of more than 70 verifiable instances of miracles in his own city of Hippo.[8]

• Reformed theologian Charles Hodge declared "there is nothing in the New Testament inconsistent with the occurrence of miracles in the postapostolic age of the Church."[9]

• Theologian Henry Clarence Thiessen, in his *Lectures in Systematic Theology*, stated: "We believe that miracles still do happen. They are not contrary even to present-day experience. All true Christians testify to the fact that God answers prayer. Indeed, they are convinced that God has wrought miracles on their behalf, or on behalf of some of their friends. They are certain that the laws of nature alone cannot account for the things which they have seen with their own eyes and experienced in their own lives. No amount of opposition on the part of unbelievers will ever persuade them to think otherwise."[10]

• Biblical scholar Gordon Clark comments: "It does not seem possible...by any direct and conclusive argument to demonstrate that miracles do not occur today. Even if they were not very numerous, an advocate of modern miracles could point out that Biblical miracles were not equally numerous in every century. Sometimes two, three, or even four centuries went by without a recorded miracle."[11]

• *The Wycliffe Bible Encyclopedia* affirms that "well-authenticated occurrences of miraculous healing have taken place in our day."[12]

Many biblical scholars are careful to make a qualification regarding the kinds of miracles they believe are occurring today. They would say that *sign* miracles (such as resurrecting people from the dead, walking on water, and turning water into wine) are no longer occurring. But there are some mighty "Grade B miracles" (providential miracles) that are occurring. I like the way apologist R. C. Sproul puts it. Consider his wise words:

> If by a miracle we mean that God is alive and well and running his world by his providence, affecting the course of human events, then by all means God is doing those things. If the question is asking whether or not God is answering prayers, then I would say emphatically, yes, God is answering prayers. If people are asking whether the providence of God is bringing extraordinary things to pass today, I would say absolutely. Does God heal people in response to prayer? I would say yes to all of those questions because I'm convinced that God is alive and well and doing all of those things....
>
> However, we may be speaking of "miracle" in the *technical* sense of an action performed against the laws of nature—God circumventing the very laws he put into motion—for example, bringing life out of death or something out of nothing, such as Jesus raising Lazarus from the dead when his body was in a state of decomposition after four days in the tomb. No, I don't think that God is doing *that* kind of miracle today.
>
> I certainly believe God *could* raise every human being in every cemetery in this world today if he wanted to. But I don't think he is performing those kinds of miracles today. The chief reason he did those things in biblical days was to certify revelation as divine—to back up what he spoke with evidence of his authority. Since we now have the Bible, however, miraculous sources of revelation are no longer necessary.[13]

So, like many other scholars, Sproul would say God in our day is doing Grade B miracles (providential miracles), but not Grade A miracles (*sign* miracles). This should not be taken to mean that God is less involved with us than He was with others in former times. Grade B miracles require supernatural power from God just as Grade A miracles do. And as I've demonstrated in this book, God is doing some powerful works in our midst today. Henry Morris holds that "providential miracles are not uncommon today."[14] Dallas theologian John Witmer says the fact that God is not doing Grade A miracles in our midst

> does not mean that God is not at work supernaturally in the world today.... In answer to believing prayer by His children God provides many things that defy human explanation—healings that are medically inexplicable, deliverances from danger that seem impossible, provision of money, food, clothing, shelter from untraceable sources. No one acquainted with the history of Dallas Theological Seminary would doubt that "Thou are the God that doest wonders" (Psalm 77:14). Christians properly call such mighty works of God miracles, but they are in a different class from the miracles of Scripture.[15]

But What About Jesus' Promise in John 14:12?

In John 14:12 Jesus said, "I tell you the truth, anyone who has faith in me will do what I have been doing. He will do even greater things than these, because I am going to the Father." Does this mean that you and I can do even more amazing and dazzling miracles than Jesus performed while He was on earth? I've heard many Christians say this must be the case. But surely this is not the intent of Jesus' words.

In this verse Jesus was simply saying His many followers would do things greater *in extent* (all over the world) and greater *in effect* (multitudes being touched by the power of God). During His short lifetime on earth, Jesus was confined in His influence to a comparatively small region of Palestine. Following His departure, His followers were able to work in widely scattered places and influence much larger numbers of human beings.[16]

Jesus in this verse was thus referring to "greater works" in terms of the whole scope of the impact of God's people and the church on the entire world throughout all history. In other words, Jesus was speaking *quantitatively*, not *qualitatively*. The works are quantitatively greater because Christ's work is multiplied through *all* His followers.[17]

It is also important to note that even these works done by Christ's followers all over the world are not done *independent* of Christ. After all, it was *He* who sent the Holy Spirit to human beings following His resurrection and ascension into heaven (John 15:26), and it is the Holy Spirit who enables believers to do these mighty works (see Acts 1:8; Romans 15:19; 1 Corinthians 12:7-11). Jesus also answers the prayers of His followers (see John 14:13,14; 16:23-26).[18] Furthermore, only those believers who are "plugged into" Him as the true vine produce abundant fruit (John 15). As Christ Himself put it, "Apart from me you can do nothing" (John 15:5).

Didn't Jesus Promise We Could Obtain Whatever We Asked For?

In Mark 11:23,24 Jesus said, "I tell you the truth, if anyone says to this mountain, 'Go, throw yourself into the sea,' and does not doubt in his heart but believes that what he says will happen, it will be done for him. Therefore I tell you, whatever you ask for in prayer, believe that you have received it, and it will be yours."

The fact is there are *limitations* on what God will give us, indicated by the broader context of Scripture. As Bible scholar David O'Brien put it, Jesus in this passage "wasn't promising a heavenly Visa card with an unlimited line of credit, or a free shopping spree in heaven's treasure house."[19]

It is important to understand that God cannot literally give us *anything*. Some things are quite impossible for God to give. For example, as Norman Geisler notes, God cannot grant a request of a creature to become God. Neither can He answer a request to approve of our sinful acts. God will not give us a stone if we ask for bread, nor will He give us a serpent if we ask for fish (Matthew 7:9,10).[20]

When the rest of Scripture is taken into consideration, there are many conditions in addition to faith placed on God's promise to answer prayer. We must abide in Him and let His Word abide in us (John 15:7). We cannot "ask with wrong motives" out of our own selfishness (James 4:3). Furthermore, we must submit our requests to the sovereign will of God. We are told "this is the confidence which we have before Him, that, if we ask anything *according to His will,* He hears us. And if we know that He hears us in whatever we ask, we know that we have the requests which we have asked from Him" (1 John 5:14,15 NASB, emphasis added)[21]

We might illustrate this with the issue of healing. It is clear from Scripture that God does not promise to heal *everyone* for whom we pray in faith, but rather the healing is subject to the will of God. I am personally aware of a number of people who have been healed of a serious illness as a result of prayer. I know of others who *were not* healed of such illnesses, and ended up dying. The apostle Paul was not healed, even though he prayed earnestly and faithfully (2 Corinthians 12:8,9). Despite the apostle Paul's divine ability to heal others (Acts 28:8,9), later he apparently could not heal either Epaphroditus (Philippians 2:25-30) or Trophimus (2 Timothy 4:20). Again, therefore, all our prayer requests should be conditioned by "if it be Your will." Sometimes God says "yes" to our requests for healing. At other times He says "no" because He has a greater purpose in mind for our lives. Either way, all of us can look forward to our resurrection bodies in which any need for "healing" will be a thing of the distant past!

The Distinction Between Miraculous "Healing" and "Miracle Healers"

Many scholars are careful to emphasize that while God can miraculously heal a person today, He does so as His own sovereign act and does not work through someone with a self-proclaimed "gift of healing" or "gift of miracles." Such gifts passed away with the apostles. Norman Geisler tells us that "the view that sign miracles ceased with the apostles does not demand that God has performed no miracles since the first century. It argues that the special *gift* of doing miraculous feats possessed by the apostles ceased once the divine origin of their message was confirmed."[22] Indeed, "while special gift miracles have ceased, the fact of miracles has not necessarily vanished. There is no evidence, however, of groups or persons who possess special gifts."[23]

This is a very important point, for there are many televangelists who claim to have this miraculous gift in our day. And the sad truth is that truckloads of people who have been proclaimed as "healed" by such healers become enormously disillusioned when they subsequently discover *they have not* in fact been healed.

When I read Chuck Swindoll's choice words regarding these alleged "faith healers," his sense of righteous indignation echoed the feelings in my own heart:

In this day of the resurgence of so-called divine
healers, my convictions may not represent a popular
position. I realize that. In no way does this mean,
however, that I do not believe God has the power to
heal...and, on unique occasions, He does do so. I
believe that with all my heart. The problem comes
when attention is focused on a person who claims
healing powers, or on the series of emotionally over-
powering events that surround a so-called healing
service. If those "divine healers" are authentic and
"anointed" miracle workers of God, why aren't they
out going floor-to-floor in hospitals and emergency
wards? Why don't they prove the truth of their ministry there...humbly...unobtrusively...free of charge?
Then I would have reason to believe they are servants
of the living God in whose lives the Spirit is consistently pouring out His power to heal.[24]

Is Healing Guaranteed in the Atonement?

There are some people today who believe Isaiah 53
teaches that physical healing is guaranteed in the atonement. I do not believe this is a correct understanding of the
passage. While *ultimate* physical healing is guaranteed in the
atonement (a healing we will enjoy in our future resurrection bodies), the healing of our bodies *while in the mortal state*
(prior to our death and resurrection) is not guaranteed in
the atonement.

It is important to note that the Hebrew word for healing
(napha) can refer not just to physical healing but also to spiritual healing. The context of Isaiah 53:4 indicates that spiritual healing is in view. In verse 5 we are clearly told, "He
was pierced through for our *transgressions,* He was crushed
for our *iniquities....*By His scourging we are healed" (NASB,
emphasis added). Because "transgressions" and "iniquities"

set the context, spiritual healing from the misery of man's sin is in view.

Further, there are numerous verses in Scripture which substantiate the view that physical healing in mortal life is not guaranteed in the atonement and that it is not always God's will to heal. As noted previously, the apostle Paul couldn't heal Timothy's stomach problem (1 Timothy 5:23), nor could he heal Trophimus at Miletus (2 Timothy 4:20) or Epaphroditus (Philippians 3:25-27). Paul spoke of "a bodily illness" he had (Galatians 4:13-15). He also suffered a "thorn in the flesh" that God allowed him to retain (2 Corinthians 12:7-9). God certainly allowed Job to go through a time of physical suffering (Job 1–2).

Neither Paul nor any of the others acted as if they thought their healing was guaranteed in the atonement. They accepted their situations and trusted in God's grace for sustenance. It is noteworthy that on one occasion Jesus indicated sickness could be for the glory of God (John 11:4).

Finally, there are numerous verses in Scripture that reveal that our physical bodies are continuously running down and suffering various ailments. Our present bodies are said to be perishable and weak (1 Corinthians 15:42-44). Paul said "our outer man is decaying" (2 Corinthians 4:16 NASB). Death and disease will be a part of the human condition until that time when we receive resurrection bodies that are immune to such frailties (1 Corinthians 15:51-55).

Today when Christians get sick, they should certainly pray for healing (see James 5:15). As well (contrary to certain televangelists), we should not be hesitant about going to the doctor. God can work a healing directly, or He can work a healing through the instrumentality of a medical professional. God never portrays doctors in a negative light. Jesus Himself said, "It is not the healthy who need a doctor, but the sick" (Matthew 9:12).

But if we *remain* sick, we must continue to trust in God and rely on His grace, as did the apostle Paul (2 Corinthians 12:9). Our attitude should be that whether we are healthy or sick, we will always rest in God's sufficiency (Philippians 4:13). God never promised to exempt us *from* situations that involve suffering, but He has promised to walk with us *through* such situations (see Psalm 23).

Miracles and the Prophetic Future

Before closing this chapter, I want to make note of the fact that a number of biblical scholars believe Scripture teaches there will be a resurgence of miracles in the end times. For example, theologian James Oliver Buswell says, "It is, in fact, the opinion of the writer that there will be another epoch of miracles in the opening stages of the eschatological complex, just preceding the 'last trumpet' of the second coming of Christ."[25] The *Wycliffe Bible Encyclopedia* likewise tells us that "it may well be that another widespread manifestation of miracles will occur in the last days before Christ's return."[26]

The book of Revelation indicates that during the future tribulation period, God will raise up two witnesses who seem to have some of the same kinds of miraculous powers that Moses and Elisha had. Revelation 11:3 tells us, "And I will give *power* to my two witnesses, and they will prophesy for 1,260 days, clothed in sackcloth" (emphasis added). We are told that "if anyone tries to harm them, fire comes from their mouths and devours their enemies" (verse 5). Further, "These men have power to shut up the sky so that it will not rain during the time they are prophesying; and they have power to turn the waters into blood and to strike the earth with every kind of plague as often as they want" (verse 6). After a time, these two prophets of God will be killed by the

Antichrist. But then, three days later, they will be raised from the dead and ascend into heaven (see Revelation 11:11,12).

Verses such as these indicate that supernatural days are not over for planet Earth. There is a period of big-time "Grade A" miracles headed our way.

What Should Our Present Attitude Be?

I realize the issue of miracles in our day is a hotly debated one. There are good Christians on both sides of the argument. I have tried to present a balanced biblical view in this chapter.

I think it is good to be reminded that we all have theological prejudices ("traditions") that we have to watch out for. J. I. Packer once wisely said:

> All Christians are at once beneficiaries and victims of tradition—beneficiaries, who receive nurturing truth in wisdom from God's faithfulness in past generations; victims, who now take for granted things that need to be questioned, thus treating as divine absolutes patterns of beliefs and behavior that should be seen as human, provisional, and relative. We are all beneficiaries of good, wise, and sound tradition and victims of poor, unwise, and unsound traditions.[27]

Some believers who have been raised in charismatic circles may have bought into an undiscerning tradition that uncritically accepts virtually all claims regarding the miraculous. On the other hand, some others raised in noncharismatic circles may have swung to the opposite side of the spectrum and may be suspicious of virtually all claims of the miraculous.

A suggested safeguard is that all traditions should be tested against the Word of God. The Bible—*not traditions and not experience*—is our sole barometer of truth. As long as we commit to following only what Scripture says, we will be kept on the right road.

Points to Ponder

- In biblical times there were some periods where miracles occurred often, but there were also many long periods where miracles seemed few and far between.

- If that was true in biblical times, then today we should certainly not expect to see one miracle after another.

- If you see some televangelist putting on a show and doing one miracle after another on nightly television, drawing attention to himself, this should raise a red flag in your mind.

- Keep in mind that if these individuals were true anointed miracle workers, they should be visiting hospital wards, healing everyone free of charge. But they are not doing this. Instead, they are putting on a show on television and raking in huge profits in the process.

- Do not be afraid to go to the doctor if you get sick. God may choose to bring a "providential miracle" your way by means of modern medicine.

~

TEN

The Case Against Miracles

Many modernists have claimed that miracles are impossible in view of the teachings of science. *Claimed* miracles are dismissed in a number of ways. Some say the observers of alleged miracles are just mistaken. Others argue that simply because we don't have a present explanation for some inexplicable event does not mean the supernatural was involved: As we grow in our understanding of the natural processes, we may come to a new *natural* understanding regarding what many observers previously thought were miraculous events. Almost all critics of miracles hold that the statistical consistency of natural law (or the "laws of nature") demonstrates that supernatural events are impossible.

Sometimes we come across references to the "miracles of modern technology." It is argued that if our ancestors witnessed some of the advances we have today—the airplane, telephone, television, laser, and the like—they would surely have considered such things miraculous. The lesson that is drawn from this assumption is that the more scientific understanding we have, the less necessity there is to believe in the supernatural.

Yet Christians respond by saying that the events
described in the Bible are *truly* miraculous. Indeed, no
matter how much science one might know, the physical resurrection of a person who has been dead and decomposing
for three days will never be *naturally* explainable. The supernatural is clearly involved in such an event.

In the present chapter, my goal will be to examine briefly
some of the major objections to miracles, and then respond
to these objections from a Christian perspective. It will be
seen that a Christian need not commit "intellectual suicide"
in maintaining a commitment to belief in supernatural miracles.

The Deist Denial of Miracles

Deism is a school of thought that grew popular in England in the seventeenth and eighteenth centuries. It sets
forth a God who created the world out of nothing but is now
completely uninvolved with the world or its events. He governs the world through unchangeable, eternal natural laws
and is in no way immanent in creation. God created the
world and the natural laws that govern the world, and since
that time has been utterly detached from its affairs.

The universe is viewed as a well-ordered machine, and
there is thus no need for any direct supernatural intervention in its affairs. Some deists suggested that God is like
someone who winds up a clock and then lets it run on its
own without interference. In their thinking, miracles would
imply that God's original creation was somehow defective
and needed some kind of intervention.

Voltaire, a French deist, believed that God oversees the
natural laws by which the universe functions, but thought it
was absurd to believe that God was providentially involved in
individual people's lives. Thomas Paine, another deist, considered God the "Great Mechanic" of creation and wrote of

that "system of principles as fixed and unalterable as those by which the universe is regulated and governed."[1] Paine emphasized that "we have never seen in our time nature go out of her course"[2]—indeed, the universe operates according to inviolable natural laws.

One famous deist was Thomas Jefferson, the main author of the American Declaration of Independence. Jefferson literally cut out from his copy of the Bible *all* the miracles of Christ in the four Gospels, and following his death this truncated version was published as *The Jefferson Bible*. This "Bible" ends without any reference to the resurrection of Jesus Christ: "Now, in the place where he was crucified, there was a garden; and in the garden a new sepulcher, wherein was never man yet laid. There laid they Jesus, and rolled a great stone to the door of the sepulcher, and departed."[3]

David Hume and the Denial of Miracles

C. S. Lewis once wrote, "If you begin by ruling out the supernatural, you will perceive no miracles."[4] He was right. The philosophy of naturalism asserts that the universe operates only according to uniform natural causes—and that it is impossible for *any* force outside the universe to intervene in the cosmos. This is an antisupernatural assumption that by definition prohibits any possibility of miracles.

David Hume was a British empiricist (meaning he believed *all* knowledge comes through the five senses) and a skeptic of the Enlightenment period. In a chapter entitled "On Miracles" in his *Enquiry Concerning Human Understanding*, he argued that, given the general experience of the uniformity of nature, miracles are highly improbable and the evidence in their favor is far from convincing.[5] He wrote: "A miracle is a violation of the laws of nature; and as a firm and unalterable experience has established these laws, the proof against a miracle, from the very nature of the fact, is as entire as any argument from experience can possibly be imagined."[6]

In his thinking, since all of one's knowledge is derived from experience, and since this experience conveys the absolute regularity of nature, any report of a miracle is much more likely to be a *false* report than a true interruption in the uniform course of nature. Hence, a report of a resurrection from the dead (for example) is in all probability a *deceptive* report.

Since Hume's time, the case against miracles has continued to grow. Many have argued that science utterly disproves the miracles of the Bible. Many others have held that the gospel writers were biased, and therefore their testimony cannot be trusted. Still others have argued that the miracles recorded in the Bible are the fantasies of ignorant people in biblical times who did not understand the laws of nature. Christians believe that such objections are easily answered.

A Defense of Miracles

There are many points a Christian can offer in response to the case against miracles described above. The place to begin is with a proper understanding of the laws of nature.

Uniformity in the Present Cosmos

Christians do not argue against the idea that there is a general uniformity in the present cosmos. As theologian John Witmer puts it,

> The Christian position is not that the universe is capricious and erratic. Christians expect the sun to rise in the east tomorrow as it always has, just as everyone else does. Christians recognize that this world is a

cosmos, an orderly system, not a chaos. More than that, Christians agree that the regularity of the universe is observable by men and expressible in principles or laws. As a result Christians do not deny the existence of what are called the laws of nature. Nor do they think that the occurrence of miracles destroys these laws or makes them inoperative.[7]

What Christians take exception to is the notion that the universe is a *self-contained closed system* with absolute laws that are inviolable. Such a position rules out any involvement of God in the world He created.

Christians believe the reason there is regularity in the universe—the reason there are "laws" that are observable in the world of nature—is because God designed it that way.[8] It is important to keep in mind, however, that the laws of nature are merely *observations* of uniformity or constancy in nature. They are not *forces* that initiate action. They are simply *descriptions* of the way nature behaves—when its course is not affected by a superior power. But God is not prohibited from taking action in the world if He so desires.

Scripture tells us that God is the sustainer and governor of the universe (Acts 14:16,17; 17:24-28). Jesus is described in the Bible as upholding "all things by the word of His power" (Hebrews 1:3 NASB) and as the one in whom "all things hold together" (Colossians 1:17). That which from a human vantage point is called the "laws of nature" is in reality nothing more than God's normal cosmos-sustaining power at work! As reformed scholar Louis Berkhof put it, these laws of nature are

> God's usual method of working in nature. It is His good pleasure to work in an orderly way and through secondary causes. But this does not mean that He cannot depart from the established order, and cannot produce an extraordinary effect, which does not

result from natural causes, by a single volition, if He deems it desirable for the end in view. When God works miracles, He produces extraordinary effects in a supernatural way.[9]

Miracles Do Not "Violate" the Laws of Nature

If one defines a miracle as a *violation* of the "absolute" laws of nature, as Hume did, then the possibility of miracles occurring seems slim. However, as theologian Charles Ryrie notes, a miracle does not contradict nature because "nature is not a self-contained whole; it is only a partial system within total reality, and a miracle is consistent within that greater system which includes the supernatural."[10]

When a miracle occurs, the laws of nature are not violated but are rather *superseded* by a higher (supernatural) manifestation of the will of God. The forces of nature are not obliterated or suspended, but are only counteracted at a particular point by a force superior to the powers of nature.[11] As the famous physicist Sir George Stokes has said, "It may be that the event which we call a miracle was brought on not by a suspension of the laws in ordinary operation, but by the super-addition of something not ordinarily in operation."[12] In other words, miracles do not go against the regular laws of cause and effect, they simply have a cause that transcends nature.[13]

Apologists Ken Boa and Larry Moody explain it this way:

> Since miracles, if they occur, are empowered by something higher than nature, they must supersede the ordinary processes or laws of nature. If you took a flying leap off the edge of a sheer cliff, the phenomenon that we call the law of gravity would surely bring you to an untimely end. But if you leaped off the same cliff in a hang glider, the results would (hopefully!) be

quite different. The principle of aerodynamics in this case overcomes the pull of gravity as long as the glider is in the air. In a similar way, the occurrence of a miracle means that a higher (supernatural) principle has overcome a lower (natural) principle for the duration of the miracle. To claim that miracles violate or contradict natural laws is just as improper as to say that the principle of aerodynamics violates the law of gravity.[14]

Boa and Moody further illustrate their point with the fictional story of a Martian who lands his spacecraft atop a building in Chicago. The Martian looks over the edge of the building and observes how people respond to traffic lights. Green lights cause people to go; yellow lights cause people to slow down; red lights cause people to stop. He observes this consistent pattern for a solid hour. All of a sudden, the Martian notices a vehicle with flashing red lights and a siren, and against all that he has thus far observed, the vehicle goes straight through the red light. "Aha!" he says, "There must be a higher law! When you have a flashing light and a loud sound, you can go through the crossing regardless of what color the light may be."[15]

What this little story is intended to illustrate is that the natural laws of the universe can be (and are on occasion) *overruled* by a higher law. The universe is not a closed system that prevents God from breaking in with the miraculous. God does not violate the laws of nature but rather *supersedes* them with a higher law. God is *over, above,* and *outside* natural law and is not bound by it.

What about scientists who claim that if such miracles were possible, it would disrupt any possibility of doing real science, since there would no longer be uniformity in the world? Well, as I argue above, there *is* uniformity in the world because God created the world that way. Miracles are unusual events that involve only a brief superseding of the natural laws. By definition, they are *out of the norm.* And unless there were a "norm" to begin with, then miracles wouldn't be possible. As apologists Peter Kreeft and Ronald Tacelli put it, "Unless there are regularities, there can be no exceptions to them."[16] Miracles are unusual, not commonplace events. A miracle is a unique event that stands out against the background of ordinary and regular occurrences. Hence, the possibility of miracles does not disrupt the possibility of doing real science.

The Problem with Hume's Argument

As noted previously, Hume argued that a "miracle is a violation of the laws of nature; and as a firm and unalterable experience has established these laws, the proof against a miracle, from the very nature of the fact, is as entire as any argument from experience can possibly be imagined."[17]

The big problem with Hume's conclusion is that there is no way that all possible "experience" can confirm his naturalistic viewpoint *unless he has access to all possible experiences in the universe, including those of the past and of the future.* And since the *finite* Hume did not have access to this much broader *(infinite)* body of knowledge, his conclusion is baseless.[18]

Theologian Henry Clarence Thiessen forcefully makes this point with an illustration based on geology:

> The...proposition that miracles are incredible because they contradict human experience, wrongly assumes that one must base *all* his beliefs on present human experience. Geologists tell of great glacial activities in the past and of the formation of seas and bays by these activities; we did not see this in our experience, but we do accept it....Miracles do not contradict human experience unless they contradict *all* human experience, that in the past as well as that in

the present. This fact leaves the door wide open for well-supported evidence as to what did happen.[19]

The reality is that we could trust very little history if we were to believe *only* those things that we have personally observed and experienced! Sadly, this is the methodology modernist critics still hold onto when it comes to the issue of miracles.

Apologists Norman L. Geisler and Ronald M. Brooks have noted that Hume essentially equates *probability* with *evidence*. Since people who die typically stay dead, a so-called miracle of resurrection is impossible. Geisler and Brooks counter, "That is like saying that you shouldn't believe it if you won the lottery because of all the thousands of people who lost. It equates evidence with probability and says that you should never believe that long shots win."[20] A miracle may be a "long shot," but long shots make good sense *when God is involved in the picture.* What is impossible with man is possible with God (Matthew 19:26).

Science Does Not *Disprove Miracles or the Bible*

Science depends upon observation and replication. Miracles, such as the incarnation and the resurrection, are by their very nature unprecedented events. No one can replicate these events in a laboratory. Hence, science simply cannot be the judge and jury as to whether or not these events occurred.

The scientific method is useful for studying nature but not *super*-nature. Just as football stars are speaking outside their field of expertise when they appear on television to tell you what razor you should buy, so scientists are speaking outside their field when they address theological issues like miracles or the resurrection.

It is also important to note that science does not involve an infallible body of absolute facts. Indeed, science historian

Thomas Kuhn, in his book *The Structure of Scientific Revolutions,* convincingly proves that science is in a constant state of change. New discoveries have consistently caused old scientific paradigms to be discarded in favor of newer paradigms. Hence, science is not some infallible judge that can simply pronounce miracles "impossible."

Actually, there is very good reason to believe in the biblical miracles. One highly pertinent factor is the brief time that elapsed between Jesus' miraculous public ministry and the publication of the gospels. It was an insufficient period for the development of miracle legends. Many eyewitnesses to Jesus' miracles would have still been alive to refute any untrue miracle accounts (see 1 Corinthians 15:6).

One must also recognize the noble character of the men who witnessed these miracles (Peter, James, and John, for example). Such men were not prone to misrepresentation, and they were willing to give up their lives rather than deny their beliefs.

There were also hostile witnesses to the miracles of Christ. For example, when Jesus raised Lazarus from the dead (John 11:45-48), none of the chief priests or Pharisees disputed the miracle. (If they could have disputed it, they would have.) Rather, their goal was simply to stop Jesus (verses 47,48). Because there were so many hostile witnesses who observed and scrutinized Christ, successful "fabrication" of miracle stories in His ministry would have been impossible.

Regarding the issue of hostile witnesses, theologian James Oliver Buswell comments:

> In the Biblical events strictly regarded as miracles, the adversaries of faith acknowledged the supernatural character of what took place. After the healing of the man "lame from his mother's womb," the rulers and elders and scribes, "beholding the man that was healed standing with them...could say nothing

against it." But they said, "...that a notable miracle hath been done by them is manifest to all them that dwell in Jerusalem, and we cannot deny it" (Acts 3:1–4:22). In the case of the miracle at Lystra (Acts 14:8-23), the pagans said, "The gods are come down to us in the likeness of men." With reference to the resurrection of Christ, Paul could ask a Roman court of law to take cognizance of an indisputable, publicly attested fact, for, said he, "This thing was not done in a corner" (Acts 26:26).[21]

Further, recall that in Acts 2:22 a bold Peter told the Jewish crowd: "Men of Israel, listen to this: Jesus of Nazareth was a man *accredited by God to you* by miracles, wonders and signs, which God did *among you* through him, *as you yourselves know*" (emphasis added). If Peter were making all this up, the huge crowd would surely have shouted Peter down. But they didn't, for they knew that what he said was true.

The Gospel Writers Were Reliable

As I noted previously, some critics of miracles say the four Gospel writers were biased in the sense that they had theological "motives." Their intent was to convince readers of Jesus' deity, we are told, and hence their historical testimony about miracles is untrustworthy.

The fallacy here is to imagine that to give an account of something one believes in passionately necessarily forces one to distort history. This is simply not true. For instance, in modern times some of the most reliable reports of the Nazi Holocaust were written by Jews who were passionately committed to seeing such genocide never repeated.

The New Testament is not made up of fairy tales but rather is based on eyewitness testimony. In 2 Peter 1:16 we read, "We did not follow cleverly invented stories when we told you about the power and coming of our Lord Jesus

Christ, but we were eyewitnesses of his majesty." First John 1:1 affirms, "That which was from the beginning, which we have heard, which we have seen with our eyes, which we have looked at and our hands have touched—this we proclaim concerning the Word of life." The historical evidence solidly supports the reliability of the New Testament writers.

Miracles Are Not the Fantasies of Ignorant People Who Did Not Understand the Laws of Nature

Such a claim is preposterous. People in biblical times *did* know enough of the laws of nature to recognize bona fide miracles. As C. S. Lewis put it,

> When St. Joseph discovered that his bride was pregnant, he was "minded to put her away." He knew enough biology for that. Otherwise, of course, he would not have regarded pregnancy as a proof of infidelity. When he accepted the Christian explanation, he regarded it as a miracle precisely because he knew enough of the laws of nature to know that this was a suspension of them.[22]

Moreover, when the disciples beheld Christ walking on the water, they were frightened—which wouldn't have been the case unless they had been aware of the laws of nature and had known this was an exception. If one has no conception of a regular order in nature, then of course one cannot notice departures from that order.[23] Nothing can be viewed as "abnormal" until one has first grasped the "norm."[24]

In keeping with this, Josh McDowell and Don Stewart tell us:

> The people living at the time of Jesus certainly knew that men born blind do not immediately receive their sight (John 9:32), that five loaves and a few fish would

not feed 5000 people (John 6:14), or that men do not walk on water (Matthew 14:25).

Doubting Thomas said, "Unless I see in his hands the print of the nails, and place my finger in the mark of the nails, and place my hand in his side, I will not believe" (John 20:25, RSV). He refused to accept the testimony of the unbelievable event of the resurrection, but changed his mind when confronted face-to-face with the resurrected Christ. Thus we are not expected to believe the ridiculous, and neither were the people of biblical times.[25]

If God Exists, Then Miracles Are Possible

The bottom line, once you get rid of all the fancy philosophical arguments against miracles, comes down to this: *If one admits the postulate of God, miracles are possible.* Paul Little writes, "Once we assume the existence of God, there is no problem with miracles, because God is by definition all-powerful."[26] Reformed scholar Charles Hodge, in his *Systematic Theology*, similarly writes: "If theism [belief in a personal Creator-God] be once admitted, then it must be admitted that the whole universe, with all that it contains and all the laws by which it is controlled, must be subject to the will of God."[27]

Really, it all goes back to the very first verse in the Bible: "In the beginning God created the heavens and the earth" (Genesis 1:1). If this verse is true (and I believe it is), then belief in miracles should be no problem—for this verse immediately establishes that an infinite and all-powerful God brought the universe into being out of nothing and that He is thus sovereign over it.

If God has the capability of calling the universe into being out of nothing, then such things as turning water into wine, walking on water, and raising people from the dead is not only possible but expected. As Norman Geisler put it so well, "If there is a God who can *act*, then there can be *acts of God*. The only way to show that miracles are impossible is to disprove the existence of God."[28] And *that* is something that cannot be done!

Points to Ponder

- There are many well-meaning Christians today who have been tainted by secular humanist thought so that their confidence in a miracle-working God is low.

- They are Christians, but in some ways they act like deists. That is, even though they have trusted in Christ for salvation, they often act as if God does not get involved in our lives today.

- A key point of discernment, then, is that while miracles happen more seldom today than in biblical times, *they should not be counted out altogether.*

- Not all miracle claims today are false. Some are real, and they bring glory to God in wonderful ways.

~

ELEVEN

Counterfeit Miracles

In the present chapter my goal is to touch on some of the counterfeit miracles and counterfeit spiritualities (which allegedly involve the miraculous) that are so popular today. The challenge is to address this subject without writing an entirely new book—for there is *so much* to choose from!

What follows should be understood as a representative sampling from a very broad pool of counterfeit miracles. I include this material with a view to emphasizing the need for discernment in dealing with claims of the miraculous.

A Course in Miracles

I begin with *A Course in Miracles,* an occultic bestseller in New Age circles. This 1200-page spiritual-psychological tome was written in the 1960s by now-deceased Jewish psychologist Helen Schucman. By a process labeled "automatic writing" (in which it is claimed that a spirit entity guides one's hand), Schucman wrote this hefty three-volume set—a 622-page textbook, a 478-page workbook, and a short manual—fully convinced that the source of the words was Jesus Himself.

Since its first publication in 1976, *A Course in Miracles* has sold around a million copies and has spawned more than 1000 study groups in the United States and abroad.[1] I visited the Bodhi Tree Bookstore in Hollywood (unquestionably one of the largest New Age bookstores in the United States), and the folks there told me this "course" is one of their hottest items *ever*.

Here are some of the first words dictated to Schucman: "This is a course in miracles. It is a required course....Miracles are everyone's right...miracles to heal the sick and raise the dead because you made sickness and death yourself, and can therefore abolish both....That is a course in mind training."[2] It would appear that by taking this course, *anyone* can create miracles. But the primary miracle this course speaks of relates to the restructuring or reprogramming of one's mind.[3]

Though this is a simple summary *(be prepared for some strange ideas),* the textbook communicates the idea that the "Son of God" was created by God in a state of "wakefulness." Later, however, the Son fell asleep and had a dream of being separate from God. In the dream, the Son denied that he was created by God, asserting instead that he created himself. This usurping of God's role as Creator marked the beginning of ego and led the Son to conceive of himself as being separate from God.

God then created and commissioned the Holy Spirit to awaken the Son. But the Son wrongly interpreted the coming of the Holy Spirit as judgment from God, because the Son thought he was guilty of usurping God's role as Creator.

The Son's ego then fragmented into myriad egos with physical bodies (that is, human beings), each believing themselves separate from each other and from God. Humanity's basic problem, then, is its belief that it is separate from God.

The solution to the problem is a rediscovery of one's Christhood. The *Course* sets out to help people attain this.[4]

As we rediscover our Christhood, a miracle begins to happen. We begin to realize sin is just an illusion, and in reality we are all perfectly innocent beings (1:375, 377-78). We also begin to realize death is just an illusion. In fact, the Jesus of the Course tells us, "There is no death, but there is a *belief* in death" (1:46). This metaphysical Jesus says "death is the central dream from which all illusions stem" (3:63).

We are not sinners in need of redemption, we are assured. Indeed, the Jesus of the *Course* explains it is "a terrible misperception that God Himself [judged] His own Son on behalf of salvation....It is so essential that all such thinking be dispelled that we must be sure that nothing of this kind remains in your mind. I was not 'punished' because you were bad" (1:32-33, 87). "Do not make the pathetic error of 'clinging to the old rugged cross'....This is not the gospel I...intended to offer you" (1:47). "Salvation is nothing more than right-mindedness," a perception that "you are one with God" (1:11,53; 2:125).

Of course, this *New Age* "course" actually embraces *age-old* lies from Satan—you can be like God, and surely you will not die (Genesis 3:4,5). Apologist Tal Brooke offers these incisive words on the sheer folly of this "course"—particularly in regard to its depiction of Jesus:

> Clearly, if *A Course in Miracles* is right, Jesus is the most misunderstood figure in history. History for two thousand years has had it wrong; the church never even got off on the right foot. And the long-promised Paraclete, the Holy Spirit, which was to guide the church through history, has not even managed to get through to Christians about their misguided understandings. They have uniformly, all of them, believed a counterfeit gospel for two thousand years. And Christ's messianic act of sacrifice on the cross, that

central historical fact of Christianity, was wasted blood and pain....For there was no real sin to atone for, and our separation from God was just an illusion all along—that is, if you believe Helen Schucman.[5]

Of course, there are no *true* miracles associated with this course. It is a satanic delusion and involves nothing but occultism. Those who put their hopes in the miracles promised by this course will only end up in spiritual deception and occultic bondage.

Creating Miracles Through "Empowerment"

How would you like to have the power to attain everything you ever wished for in life? How would you like to be able to create your own miracles? You can, according to David Gershon and Gail Straub. In their blockbuster New Age book, *Empowerment: The Art of Creating Your Life as You Want It,* Gershon and Straub tell us that "empowerment" is the key, for this will give you the miraculous ability to create your own reality by the power of your own mind. What "manifests" in your life will be a direct result of the thoughts you affirm—either on a conscious or unconscious level.

Gershon and Straub's central idea is that empowerment "will free you from boundaries that have limited you in the past and show you your power to shape your own destiny. On this journey you will learn the art of creating your life as you want it."[6]

The authors explain their theory this way:

Of all the knowledge pertaining to the evolution of the human condition that has come to light in this extraordinary time in which we live, none is more promising than this idea: *We make and shape our character and the conditions of our life by what we think.* What

> you think and believe will manifest in your life. By becoming adept at intelligently *directing* your thought, you can become adept at creating the life that you want. You can take charge of your destiny.[7]

Gershon and Straub note that "we can't avoid creating our reality; each time we think a thought we are creating it. Every belief we hold is shaping what we experience in our life."[8] In view of this, "if we accept the basic premise that our thoughts create our reality, it means that we need to take responsibility for creating *all* of our reality—the parts we like and the parts we don't like."[9]

The authors then offer us a game plan for achieving empowerment that focuses on making effective use of *affirmations* (positive self-talk) and *visualizations* (mental pictures of what you want to create). This is the way to bring about miraculous changes in one's life. By using these affirmations and visualizations, Gershon and Straub assure us we will attract the worldly "nutrients" needed to have our "mental seed" grow to "fruition."[10]

This New Age team also provides a list of "limiting beliefs" and accompanying "turnarounds." By affirming the turnarounds, we are told, we can dispose of unhealthy beliefs that limit us. Here are a few examples:

Limiting Belief: God is a male figure with a lot of power who will punish me if I don't do the right thing.

Turnaround: I create God as a loving, kind, playful, wise, powerful friend. We play together co-creating the universe.[11]

Limiting Belief: Spirituality means giving over control of my life to some higher power that's outside of me.

Turnaround: God's will is my own highest consciousness in this moment.[12]

Limiting Belief: To be spiritual I must follow a code of conduct laid out by a religion/guru/writer of a spiritual book.

Turnaround: My spirituality grows out of my own self-knowledge. I trust it and found my actions upon it.[13]

Limiting Belief: The world is full of corrupt, evil people who are leading it down a road of destruction.

Turnaround: I take responsibility to create the world as a beautiful and sacred place filled with beings committed to their own and the planet's evolution.[14]

By using positive affirmations such as these—combined with visualization—our thoughts can allegedly begin to change the reality around us. By using our minds, we have true *power.* By using our minds, we can make miraculous changes in our lives.

There are many ways I could critique this idea of creating one's reality by the power of the mind. Here I simply want to focus attention on one of the profound moral implications of this teaching.

As I noted earlier, Gershon and Straub say that if we accept the basic premise that our thoughts create our reality, it means that we need to take responsibility for creating *all* of our reality—*the parts we like and the parts we don't like.*[15] The point I want to make in response to this is that if man creates his own reality, then he cannot legitimately condemn individuals who inflict evil upon others.

For example, one must conclude that the millions of Jews who were executed under Hitler's regime *created their own reality.* Hence, Hitler's actions cannot be condemned as ethically wrong, since Hitler was only part of a reality that the Jews themselves created. Similarly, one cannot condemn terrorists who blow up passenger jets, because the people on those jets create their own reality. The moral implications of this theory show its ultimate absurdity.

I must also point out that Gershon and Straub's mind-over-matter techniques are blatantly occultic and non-Christian. And, like other New Agers, they deny wholesale that man (including his imagination) is *fallen* (Genesis 6:5). Thus they are blinded to the reality that they are using faulty equipment that can lead them astray. How much better it is to trust in the sure promises of a loving (and miraculous) God for provisions in life rather than having to depend on one's visualizing prowess (see Matthew 6:30).

The Omnipotence of Man

Shirley MacLaine once said, "You are unlimited. You just don't realize it."[16] British New Ager George Trevelyan said that each human being is "an eternal droplet of the Divine Ocean, and that potentially it can evolve into a being who can be a *co-creator* with God."[17] The New Age gospel of Levi Dowling—*The Aquarian Gospel of Jesus the Christ*—maintains that Jesus Himself taught that human beings have unlimited potential and can create their own miracles.

Indeed, the Jesus of this book tells us: "Because I have the power to do these things is nothing strange. All men may gain the power to do these things....So man is God on earth, and he who honors God must honor man."[18] Dowling also cites Jesus as saying: "I came to show the possibilities of man; what I have done all men may do, and what I am all men shall be."[19] And again, "What I can do all men can do. Go preach the gospel of the omnipotence of man."[20]

Of course, man is not an omnipotent god who can create his own miracles. Such an assertion is as ridiculous as it is comical. If it were true (hypothetically) that human beings were omnipotent gods, then we would expect them to display qualities similar to those known to be true of God. However, when we compare the attributes of humankind with those of God, we find more than ample testimony for the truth of Paul's statement in Romans 3:23 that human beings "fall short of the glory of God." Consider the following:

- God is all-knowing (Isaiah 40:13,14), but man is limited in knowledge (Job 38:4).

- God is all-powerful (Revelation 19:6), but man is weak (Hebrews 4:15).

- God is everywhere-present (Psalm 139:7-12), but man is confined to one single space at a time (John 1:50).

- God is holy (1 John 1:5), but even man's "righteous" deeds are as filthy garments before God (Isaiah 64:6).

- God is eternal (Psalm 90:2), but man was created at a point in time (Genesis 1:1,26,27).

- God is truth (John 14:6), but man's heart is deceitful above all else (Jeremiah 17:9).

- God is characterized by justice (Acts 17:31), but man is lawless (1 John 3:4; see also Romans 3:23).

- God is love (Ephesians 2:4,5), but man is plagued with numerous vices, such as jealousy and strife (1 Corinthians 3:3).

If man is a god, *one could never tell it by his attributes!*

Man's ignorance of his alleged divinity also proves he is not God. If human beings are essentially God, and if God is an infinite and changeless being, then how is it possible for man (if he is a manifestation of divinity) to go through a changing process of enlightenment by which he discovers his divinity? "The fact that a man 'comes to realize' he is God proves that he is not God. If he were God he would never have passed from a state of unenlightenment to a state of enlightenment as to who he is."[21] To put it another way, "God cannot bud. He cannot blossom. God has always been in full bloom. That is, God is and always has been God."[22]

So, I say again: *Man is not an omnipotent god of miracles.* This is deluded thinking at its worst.

"Name" and "Claim" Your Own Miracle: The Word-Faith Movement

"Name it and claim it" has become a household phrase in millions of homes across America. Why? Because Word-Faith teachers perpetually teach this doctrine on national television. Just about every night one can tune in and learn how to gain health or wealth by following the prosperity formulas of Word-Faith teachers. These formulas, however, have more in common with cultic metaphysics than with Christianity.

Word-Faith teachers are indebted to Phineas P. Quimby's school of metaphysical thought, which came to be known as "New Thought." Quimby taught his followers they could create their own reality through the power of "positive affirmation." (David Gershon and Gail Straub, discussed previously in this chapter, were also fans of Quimby.) By using creative visualization, one can allegedly transform intangible images into tangible existence.[23]

In reality, the Word-Faith teachers set forth a gospel of greed and avarice. The primary "miracle" in this gospel is the miracle of a fat wallet. This is not the gospel of the Bible (1 Corinthians 15:1-4). Their gospel is commonly known as the "prosperity gospel"—which sets forth the idea that it is God's will that all Christians be materially wealthy. Following are some of the key elements of this deviant theology:

God Desires His Children to Be Wealthy.
We are told God not only wants to deliver believers from poverty, but He wants His children to eat the best food, wear the best clothing, drive the best cars, and have the best of everything.[24]

It Is a Sin to be Poor.
Word-Faith teachers often communicate the idea that it is sinful to be in a state of poverty.[25] One wonders whether

such Word-Faith teachers have read their Bibles recently! Did not Jesus say, "Blessed are the poor" (Luke 6:20)?

Jesus Is Our Example, and He Was Not Poor.

Jesus' alleged wealth is a favorite theme among Word-Faith teachers.[26] We are told that Jesus wore designer clothes[27] and had a very big house.[28] He also had enough money that he had a treasurer.[29] Of course, there are no Scripture verses that teach any of this.

God Sets Forth Laws of Prosperity in the Bible.

Word-Faith teachers say there are certain laws governing prosperity in God's Word. *Faith* causes these laws to function. The "success formulas" in the Word of God produce miraculous financial results when used as directed.[30]

Positive Confession Is the Key to Gaining Wealth.

If we want wealth, all we have to do is *speak* it into existence. That's the key to a financial miracle. We are told that *confession brings possession.*[31]

Giving Money to God's Work Can Yield a Hundredfold Increase.

Based on a complete distortion of Mark 10:30, we are told we will receive a miraculous hundredfold return when we give money to ministries.[32] We are assured if we invest heavily in God, the financial returns will be staggering.[33] (One wonders why Word-Faith teachers do not give all *their* money to ministries in order to attain a hundredfold return. Instead, they constantly appeal for money on television.)

Christians Are Enticed.

Tragically, millions of Christians are being enticed into the cultic Word-Faith movement through this gospel of prosperity. Christians are being lured into seeking what is on the *Master's table* rather than seeking the *Master's face.*

I am personally aware of elderly Christians who have given their life savings to television ministries in hope of bringing financial blessing on themselves in their final years. Instead, they end up in bankruptcy. It is impossible to calculate just how many lives have been shattered as a result of this deviant, cruel theology that promises "miracle money."

It is not necessary to biblically refute each of the above elements of the prosperity message: This has been done more than adequately in other books.[34] However, a brief perusal of a few key Scripture passages relating to the overall perspective God desires us to have toward money and riches presents a helpful contrast to the Word-Faith distortions.

First, let's recognize that God does not condemn possessions or riches *per se*. It is not a sin to be wealthy! (Some very godly people in the Bible—Abraham and Job, for example—were quite wealthy.) But God does condemn a *love* of possessions or riches (Luke 16:13; 1 Timothy 6:10; Hebrews 13:5). A love of material things is a sure sign that a person is living according to a temporal perspective, not an eternal perspective. If you're looking for *that* kind of miracle, you've got your head *(and your heart)* in the wrong place.

Scripture tells us that a love of money and riches leads to sure destruction. The apostle Paul flatly stated that "people who want to get rich fall into temptation and a trap and into many foolish and harmful desires that plunge men into ruin and destruction" (1 Timothy 6:9).

Jesus understandably warned His followers: "Watch out! Be on your guard against all kinds of greed; a man's life does not consist in the abundance of his possessions" (Luke 12:15). He then urged His followers to have an eternal perspective, exhorting: "Do not store up for yourselves treasures on earth, where moth and rust destroy, and where thieves break in and steal. But store up for yourselves treasures in heaven" (Matthew 6:19,20; see also John 6:27).

Jesus urged: "Seek first his kingdom and his righteousness, and all these things will be given to you as well" (Matthew 6:33). In other words, living for God in a righteous way should be our top priority. When we do this, we can rest assured God will provide us with the necessities of life.

And if God in His sovereign grace should bless us with material wealth, as He did Abraham and Job, we can use it for His glory and for the extension of His kingdom. We can use such wealth as a channel of blessing for others.

Our attitude should be whether we are rich or poor (or somewhere in between), we are simply stewards of what God has provided us. Our attitude should mirror that of the apostle Paul, who said: "I know what it is to be in need, and I know what it is to have plenty. I have learned the secret of being content in any and every situation, whether well fed or hungry, whether living in plenty or in want. I can do everything through him who gives me strength" (Philippians 4:12,13).

Miracles and the Apparitions of Mary

According to recent estimates, Mary (the mother of Jesus) has appeared to people over 21,000 times since her death in the first century.[35] In many cases, there are reports of miracles and divine healings that accompany the appearances. The most recent series of alleged appearances have taken place in Medjugorje in Bosnia-Herzegovina.

Catholics tell us that Mary has appeared to people throughout history, including in Guadalupe, Mexico, 1531; Rue de Bac, France, 1830; Salette, France, 1846; Lourdes, France, 1858; Fatima, Portugal, 1917; Beauraing, Belgium, 1933; Banneau, Belgium, 1933; and Medjugorje, 1981. To date, over 10 million Catholics have traveled to Medjugorje to witness the appearances of Mary since they began in June of 1981. In these appearances, Mary speaks of distinctly

Catholic doctrines—calling people to perform acts of penance and to pray the rosary. She also asks that people express greater devotion to her.

Apologists Elliot Miller and Ken Samples summarize the alleged miraculous activity that has taken place at Medjugorje:

> There have…allegedly been various signs and miracles that accompany the already supernatural apparitions in Medjugorje. The most popular is undoubtedly the "Miracle of the Sun" phenomenon. Rene Laurentin, an eminent Marian scholar, stated that "on numerous occasions, thousands have witnessed the sun change colors, spin, become a silver disc, throb and pulsate in the sky, and throw off a rainbow of colors.…"
>
> Most pilgrims claim that a part of the miracle is that they are able to observe the sun for several minutes without suffering any damage to their eyes.…
>
> In addition to the phenomena of the sun, unusual things have reportedly taken place in connection with a large cross at the top of Mount Krizevac, the highest peak in the area. This twenty-foot cement cross, which overlooks Medjugorje, was built in 1933 to commemorate the nineteen-hundredth year since Christ's death and resurrection. Some pilgrims have testified that they have seen the arms of the cross mysteriously spin. Others say that the cross frequently becomes a column of light more intense than a neon cross. Still others claim that they have seen the concrete cross disappear completely before their very eyes. It has also been reported that the word *mir* (the Croatian word for peace) has appeared in bright letters in the sky above the cross.
>
> Other extraordinary events have been reported, including rosaries allegedly turning a gold or copper color, fires on the hillside with nothing being scorched,

images of Jesus and Mary seen in the sky, and
numerous claims to physical healings.[36]

Personally, I do not believe that a single *genuine* appearance of the Virgin Mary has ever taken place. I say this not
because I have anything against Mary (I do not—for she is
truly blessed among women—see Luke 1:28). I say this
because of the scriptural teaching that contact with the dead
in any form is forbidden by God (Deuteronomy 18:11). We
should not expect that God would allow Mary to do something that He has explicitly forbidden. From a scriptural perspective, we will be reunited with the dead *only* at the second
coming of Christ (see 1 Thessalonians 4:13-17), and not
before.

Some reputable evangelical scholars who have studied
the issue have suggested there may be any number of explanations of people's claims to have seen Mary. There may be
some human deception playing a role; there could be some
psychological projection or hallucination; or there could be
some kind of physical or natural scientific cause.[37] However,
because the nature of these apparitions (contact with the
dead) goes against what is taught in Scripture, *and* because
unbiblical doctrines (such as the rosary) are taught by the
"Mary" who appears, *if* there is any kind of supernatural element involved, that element is likely satanic or demonic.

Scripture indicates that Satan "masquerades as an angel
of light" (2 Corinthians 11:14,15). He has the ability to perform "counterfeit miracles, signs and wonders" (2 Thessalonians 2:9,10). In the end times he will inspire false Christs
and false prophets who will "perform great signs and miracles to deceive even the elect—if that were possible"
(Matthew 24:24). We are told in the book of Revelation that
the "beast" and the "false prophet"—both inspired by
Satan—will perform "great signs," even making "fire come
down out of heaven to the earth in the presence of men"
(Revelation 13:13 NASB).

In view of this, there is no doubt that Satan has the ability to counterfeit appearances of the Virgin Mary. Certainly he is more than happy to do so if the end result is that many people end up deceived by such doctrines as Mariolatry, penance, purgatory, the veneration of saints, and the like.

Certainly the miracles alleged to have occurred in Medjugorje are of a different type than those reported in the Bible. After all, where do you read in the Bible of spinning crosses and a dancing sun? Jesus performed miracles that actually *benefited* people and never engaged in miracles simply for the sake of marvel. Furthermore, when Jesus performed a miracle, virtually everyone in the vicinity of Jesus recognized that a miracle had occurred. Not so at Medjugorje. Often only a few people see one of these phenomena, while others who are present see nothing.

I might also mention, in closing, that *The New England Journal of Medicine* featured an article on people who have suffered serious eye damage from watching the sun while in Medjugorje. In fact, it is happening so often these days that doctors have coined the term "Medjugorje affliction" to describe it.[38] The "miracles" at Medjugorje can be dangerous!

Reader Beware

There are all kinds of claims being made by people all over the world about various kinds of miracles. But not everything that is claimed to be a miracle is in fact a true miracle. This chapter has dealt only with the "tip of the iceberg" of counterfeit miracles in our world. So—reader beware! Never forget to test all things against Scripture, our only true standard of truth (1 Thessalonians 5:21).

Points to Ponder

- True miracles are always done in *God's* power.

- Many people today teach that you can become *your own* god, create *your own* reality, and bring about *your own* miracles. This is not of God. It is of Satan, the father of lies (John 8:44).

- Many so-called miracles today are based on the power of the human mind (especially among New Agers, the metaphysical cults, and Word-Faith proponents). You can allegedly "name it and claim it." This is *not* God at work. This is metaphysical occultism.

- Beware of "miracles" relating to promises of prosperity. Do not be duped by the "hundred-fold return" swindle. This is *not* of God.

~

TWELVE

Can the Devil Perform Miracles?

The evidence in the Bible for the existence and activity of Satan and demons is formidable. Seven books in the Old Testament specifically teach the reality of Satan (Genesis, 1 Chronicles, Job, Psalms, Isaiah, Ezekiel, and Zechariah). Every New Testament writer and 19 of the New Testament books make specific reference to him (for example, Matthew 4:10; 12:26; Mark 1:13; 3:23,26; 4:15; Luke 11:18; 22:3; John 13:27). Jesus refers to Satan some 25 times.

Throughout church history, some people have claimed Satan is not a real person—an idea no doubt inspired by Satan himself. After all, if there is no real "enemy," then there certainly is no need to prepare a defense against him. And if there is no preparation for defense, then the enemy can attack at will and work his evil while remaining incognito.

The Scriptures are just as definite about Satan's existence as God's existence. The Scriptures reveal that Satan is both a fallen angel *and* a genuine person. How do we know he is a person? For one thing, Satan has all the attributes of personality—including *mind* (2 Corinthians 11:3), *emotions* (Revelation 12:17; Job 1:9; 2:4), and *will* (Isaiah 14:12-14; 2 Timothy 2:26). Not only that, but personal pronouns are used to describe him in the Bible (Job 1; Matthew 4:1-11). As well, Satan performs personal actions (Matthew 4:1-11; John 8:44; 1 John 3:8; Jude 9).

The Scriptures portray Satan as a created being who—though powerful and capable of performing "lying signs and wonders" (2 Thessalonians 2:9)—has definite limitations. Satan does not possess attributes that belong to God alone, such as *omnipresence* (being everywhere-present), *omnipotence* (being all-powerful), and *omniscience* (being all-knowing). Satan is a *creature*, and as a creature he is lesser than (and is responsible to) the Creator. Satan can only be in one place at one time; his strength, though great, is limited; and his knowledge, though great, is limited.

Satan, though possessing creaturely limitations, is nevertheless pictured in Scripture as being extremely powerful and influential in the world. He is called the "ruler of this world" (John 12:31 NASB), "the god of this world" (2 Corinthians 4:4 NASB), and the "prince of the power of the air" (Ephesians 2:2 NASB). He is also said to deceive the whole world (Revelation 12:9; 20:3). He is portrayed as having power in the governmental realm (Matthew 4:8,9; 2 Corinthians 4:4), the physical realm (Luke 13:11,16; Acts 10:38), the angelic realm (Jude 9; Ephesians 6:11,12), and the ecclesiastical (church) realm (Revelation 2:9; 3:9). Clearly Satan is a being that Christians should be very concerned about.

Satan's Vast Experience

It is critical that Christians realize Satan has vast experience in bringing human beings down. In fact, his experience is far greater than that of any human being. As Charles Ryrie puts it,

> By his very longevity Satan has acquired a breadth and depth of experience which he matches against the limited knowledge of man. He has observed... believers in every conceivable situation, thus enabling him to predict with accuracy how we will respond to circumstances. Although Satan is not omniscient, his wide experience and observation of man throughout his entire history on earth give him knowledge which is far superior to anything any man could have.[1]

Because of his vast experience, Satan has acquired many wiles and learned many tricks to deceive human beings. Some of his deceitful tricks no doubt relate to the counterfeit miracles he inspires. *Christians are therefore urged to beware* (1 Peter 5:8; 2 Corinthians 2:11).

Satan as the "Ape" of God

It was Augustine who called the Devil *Simius Dei*—"the ape of God." Satan is the great counterfeiter.[2] He mimics God in many ways. A primary tactic Satan uses to attack God and His program in general is to offer a counterfeit kingdom and program.[3] This is hinted at in 2 Corinthians 11:14, which makes reference to Satan *masquerading* as an "angel of light."

In what ways does Satan act as "the ape of God"? Consider the following:

- Satan has his own *church*—the "synagogue of Satan" (Revelation 2:9).

- Satan has his own *ministers*—ministers of darkness that bring false sermons (2 Corinthians 11:4,5).

- Satan has formulated his own *system of theology*—called "doctrines of demons" (1 Timothy 4:1 NASB; Revelation 2:24).

- Satan's ministers proclaim a counterfeit *gospel*—"a gospel other than the one we preached to you" (Galatians 1:7,8).

- Satan has his own *throne* (Revelation 13:2) and his own worshipers (13:4).

- Satan inspires *false Christs* and self-constituted messiahs (Matthew 24:4,5).

- Satan employs *false teachers* who bring in "destructive heresies" (2 Peter 2:1).

- Satan sends out *false prophets* (Matthew 24:11).

- Satan sponsors *false apostles* who imitate the true ones (2 Corinthians 11:13).

In view of this mimicking of God by Satan, one theologian has concluded that "Satan's plan and purposes have been, are, and always will be to seek to establish a rival rule to God's kingdom. He is promoting a system of which he is the head and which stands in opposition to God and His rule in the universe."[4]

Scripture indicates that Satan as the "ape of God" performs counterfeit signs and wonders. Indeed, 2 Thessalonians 2:9 tells us, "The coming of the lawless one will be in accordance with the work of Satan displayed in all kinds of counterfeit miracles, signs and wonders."

The World of Demons—"Hell's Angels"

Satan is joined in his work by a vast host of demons. Demons are "fallen angels" and are portrayed in Scripture as evil and wicked. They are defined as "unclean spirits" (Matthew 10:1 NASB), "evil spirits" (Luke 7:21), and "spiritual forces of wickedness" (Ephesians 6:12 NASB). All these terms point to the immoral nature of demons.[5]

What kinds of wicked things do demons do? Among many other things, Scripture portrays them as inflicting physical diseases on people (such as *dumbness,* Matthew 9:33; *blindness,* 12:22; and *epilepsy,* 17:15-18). They also afflict people with mental disorders (Mark 5:4,5; 9:22; Luke 8:27-29; 9:37-42). They cause people to be self-destructive (Mark 5:5; Luke 9:42). They are even responsible for the deaths of some people (Revelation 9:14-19).

Of course, we must be careful to note that even though demons can cause physical illnesses, Scripture draws a distinction between natural illnesses and demon-caused illnesses (Matthew 4:24; Mark 1:32; Luke 7:21; 9:1; Acts 5:16). Theologian Millard J. Erickson notes there are no demons involved in the case of quite a few of Christ's miraculous healings in the New Testament. "In Matthew, for example, no mention is made of demon exorcism in the case of the healing of the centurion's servant (8:5-13), the woman with the hemorrhage of 12 years' duration (9:19,20), the two blind men (9:27-30), the man with the withered hand (12:9-14), and those who touched the fringe of Jesus' garment (14:35,36)."[6] Hence, every time you get sick you must not presume you are being afflicted by a demon.

Presently there are two classes or groups of demons. One group of demons is free and active in opposing God and His people (Ephesians 2:1-3). The other group of demons is confined. Charles Ryrie notes

> of those who are confined, some are temporarily so, while others are permanently confined in Tartarus (2 Peter 2:4 and Jude 6). The Greeks thought of Tartarus as a place of punishment lower than Hades. Those temporarily confined are in the abyss (Luke 8:31; Revelation 9:1-3,11), some apparently consigned there to await final judgment, while others will

be loosed to be active on the earth [during the future seven-year tribulation period] (verses 1-3,11,14; 16:14).[7]

Why are some fallen angels (demons) permanently confined? It seems reasonable to assume they are being punished for some sin other than the original rebellion against God. Some theologians believe these angels are guilty of the unnatural sin mentioned in Genesis 6:2-4 and, because of the gross depravity of this sin, they are permanently confined to Tartarus.[8]

The Work of Fallen Angels Among Unbelievers

Second Corinthians 4:4 states that Satan blinds the minds of unbelievers to the truth of the gospel. This passage indicates that Satan inhibits the unbeliever's ability to think or reason properly in regard to spiritual matters.[9] It seems that one of the ways Satan does this is by leading people to think that any way to heaven is as acceptable as another. In other words, Satan promotes the idea that one doesn't need to believe in Jesus Christ as the *only* means to salvation.

Satan also seeks to snatch the Word of God from the hearts of unbelievers when they hear it (Luke 8:12). Demons, under Satan's lead, seek to disseminate false doctrine (1 Timothy 4:1). As well, they wield influence over false prophets (1 John 4:1-4) and seek to turn people to the worship of idols (see Leviticus 17:7; Deuteronomy 32:17; Psalm 106:36-38). In short, fallen angels do all they can to spread spiritual deception.

The Work of Fallen Angels Among Believers

Fallen angels are also very active in seeking to harm believers in various ways. For example:

- Satan tempts believers to sin (1 Corinthians 7:5; 1 Thessalonians 3:5).

- Satan tempts believers to lie (Acts 5:3).

- Satan tempts believers to commit sexually immoral acts (1 Corinthians 7:5).

- Satan accuses and slanders believers (Revelation 12:10).

- Satan hinders the work of believers in any way he can (1 Thessalonians 2:18).

- Satan and demons seek to wage war against and *defeat* believers (Ephesians 6:11,12).

- Satan sows tares (weeds) among believers (Matthew 13:38,39).

- Satan incites persecutions against believers (Revelation 2:10).

- Demons hinder answers to the prayers of believers (Daniel 10:12-20).

- Satan is said to oppose Christians with the ferociousness of a hungry lion (1 Peter 5:8).

- Satan seeks to plant doubt in the minds of believers (Genesis 3:1-5).

- Satan seeks to foster spiritual pride in the hearts of Christians (1 Timothy 3:6).

- Satan seeks to lead believers away from "the simplicity and purity of devotion to Christ" (2 Corinthians 11:3 NASB).

- Demons seek to instigate jealousy and factions among believers (James 3:13-16).

- Demons would separate the believer from Christ if they could (Romans 8:38,39).

- Demons cooperate with Satan in working against believers (Matthew 25:41; Ephesians 6:12; Revelation 12:7-12).

What About Miracles?

Although Satan has great spiritual powers, there is a gigantic difference between the power of the devil and the power of God. First, God is infinite in power (omnipotent); the devil (like demons) is finite and limited. Second, only God can create life (Genesis 1:1,21; Deuteronomy 32:39); the devil cannot (see Exodus 8:19). Only God can truly raise the dead (John 10:18; Revelation 1:18); the devil cannot, though he will one day give "breath" (animation) to the idolatrous *image* of the Antichrist (Revelation 13:15).

The devil has great power to deceive people (Revelation 12:9), to oppress those who yield to him, and even to possess them (Acts 16:16). He is a master magician and a super scientist. And with his vast knowledge of God, man, and the universe, he is able to perform "*counterfeit* miracles, signs and wonders" (2 Thessalonians 2:9 emphasis added; see also Revelation 13:13,14). Simon the sorcerer in the city of Samaria amazed people with his Satan-inspired magic (Acts 8:9-11), but the miracles accomplished through Philip were *much, much greater* (Acts 8:13). The devil's *counterfeit* miracles do not compete with God's *true* miracles.

Perhaps the best illustration of Satan's counterfeit wonders is found in the book of Exodus. In Exodus 7:10, for example, we read that Aaron's rod was turned into a snake by the power of God. Then, according to verse 11, Pharaoh "summoned wise men and sorcerers, and the Egyptian magicians also did the same things by their secret arts." The purpose of these acts, of course, was to convince Pharaoh his magicians possessed as much power as Moses and Aaron, and it was not necessary for Pharaoh to yield to their request to let Israel go. The magicians' arts worked, *at least for the first three encounters* (Aaron's rod, the plague of blood, and the plague of frogs). However, when Moses and Aaron by the power of God brought forth lice from the sand, the magicians were not able to counterfeit this miracle. They could only exclaim, "This is the finger of God" (Exodus 8:19).

Biblical scholars differ as to whether Satan just does convincing tricks or genuine (albeit limited) miraculous works. Some scholars assert that the feats of Egypt's magicians, inspired by Satan, were done by sleight of hand. Perhaps the magicians had enchanted the snakes so that they became stiff and appeared to be rods. When cast down upon the floor, they came out of their trance and began to move. It is suggested that Satan is the "father of lies" (John 8:44), Satan very well may have been pulling some kind of trick instead of performing a true miracle.

Other scholars say these were supernatural and miraculous acts of Satan, who actually did turn the rods of the magicians into snakes. Dr. Henry Morris, for example, believes the devil and demons may be able to perform some "Grade B" miracles. They may be capable of "great juggling of the world's natural processes...."[10]

Still others, like theologian John Witmer, believe Satan *sometimes* does tricks and *sometimes* does supernatural (albeit limited) miraculous works:

> Some of these spectacles are mere trickery, spurious miracles. Others of them are truly supernatural events, but Satanic in origin and power, not divine. Remember that the devil showed the Lord Jesus "all

the kingdoms of the world in a moment of time"
(Luke 4:5 NASB) and is able to transform himself into
"an angel of light" (2 Corinthians 11:14).[11]

Reformed theologian Charles Hodge, in his *Systematic Theology*, notes that whether or not Satan can perform a miracle hinges on how one defines "miracle":

> The question is, Are they to be regarded as *true* miracles? The answer to this question depends on the meaning of the word. If by a miracle we mean any event transcending the efficiency of physical causes and the power of man, then they are miracles. But if we adhere to the definition...which requires that the event be produced *by the immediate power of God,* they of course are not miracles.[12]

Whether or not Satan has the ability to perform a few limited "Grade B" miracles or whether his works are just impressive tricks, the scriptural evidence is undeniably clear that heavy-duty "Grade A" miracles can be performed *only* by God. Only God can fully control and supersede the natural laws He Himself created, though on one occasion He did grant Satan the power to bring a whirlwind on Job's family (Job 1:19). As the account of Job illustrates, all the power the devil has is granted him by God and is *carefully limited and monitored* (see Job 1:10-12). In other words, Satan is "on a leash." Satan's *finite* power is under the control of God's *infinite* power.

Discerning Between God's Miracles and Satan's Lying Wonders

Scripture gives us the key to discerning between the true miracles of God and the lying wonders of Satan. We find this key summarized in Deuteronomy 13:1-3:

> If a prophet, or one who foretells by dreams, appears
> among you and announces to you a miraculous sign
> or wonder, and if the sign or wonder of which he has
> spoken takes place, and he says, "Let us follow other
> gods" (gods you have not known) "and let us worship
> them," you must not listen to the words of that
> prophet or dreamer. The LORD your God is testing
> you to find out whether you love him with all your
> heart and with all your soul.

What this means is if a person claiming to perform a miracle of God is teaching false doctrine, we may assume *without hesitation* that this person's "miracle" is not done in the power of God but is a lying wonder rooted in Satan. Norman Geisler notes there are a variety of false teachings or activities that might be connected to a "counterfeit miracle" rooted in Satan:

> Numerous evils are mentioned in the Bible, such as
> idolatry (1 Corinthians 10:19), immorality (Ephesians
> 2:3), divination (Deuteronomy 18:10), false prophe-
> cies (Deuteronomy 18:22), occult activity (Deuter-
> onomy 18:14), worshiping other gods (Deuteronomy
> 13:1,2), deceptive activity (2 Thessalonians 2:9), con-
> tacting the dead (Deuteronomy 18:11,12), messages
> contrary to those revealed through true prophets
> (Galatians 1:8), and prophecies that do not center on
> Jesus Christ (Revelation 19:10).[13]

If the "miracle" confirms or supports any of the evils listed above, it *cannot* be from the God of truth. God's miracles are never connected to the kingdom of darkness.[14]

It is interesting to note that whenever a serious question arose in biblical days as to which events were of God and which were of the devil, a contest would often follow in which God's power triumphed over that of the devil. For example, God was clearly the victor in the contest between

Him and the magicians of Egypt (recall, for example, that Aaron's snake swallowed those of the Egyptian sorcerers, Exodus 7:10-12). Likewise, Elijah was triumphant over Baal's prophets on Mount Carmel, when fire came down from heaven and consumed the sacrifices (1 Kings 18).[15]

Regardless of any powers the devil and his demons may seem to have, we can rest secure in the fact that *Christ has defeated them* (Hebrews 2:14,15; Colossians 2:15). Christ has provided all that is necessary for Christians to be victorious over all demonic forces (Ephesians 4:4-11; 1 John 4:4).

Points to Ponder

- False doctrine or false practices connected with a person's performing an alleged miracle are a sure indicator that the "miracle" cannot be of the one true God (Deuteronomy 13:1-3).

- Beware that Satan can perform astonishing conjuring tricks and possibly some "Grade B" counterfeit miracles. In view of this, do not assume that, every time someone claims something to be a "miracle," it is necessarily of God. Use the "points" in this book to test the miracle against God's Word.

~

THIRTEEN

Miracles of New Age "Energetic Medicine"

Not long ago, I came across an article in a New Age magazine about a man who pulled a ligament in his foot during a workout. It caused pain through his entire leg. With considerable effort he made his way to an orthopedist, who informed him he might require some serious surgery—and it might take a long time to recover. Not liking that option, the man decided on a whim to visit a New Age health practitioner. This practitioner specialized in a "healing art" known as the "therapeutic touch."

The New Age health practitioner did a quick exam and then went through a series of motions, maneuvering his hands up and down the injured man's body, about two or three inches above his skin. He appeared to be manipulating and smoothing out some kind of invisible energy or force—much like smoothing a wrinkle out of a tablecloth. At one point, the practitioner shook his hands off to the side, as if he were shaking off excess energy no longer needed. He then said to the man, "Go ahead and try to walk now."

To his astonishment, the injured man felt no pain at all. It was a "miracle." He was healed! He asked the New Age practitioner what he had done. The practitioner responded that our material bodies are just patterns of energy held together by our mental consciousness. Sometimes energy blockages occur in the body, and when that happens, we experience physical symptoms. By relieving and getting rid of those energy blockages, we are restored to health. Thus the man's injured foot no longer felt pain once the blocked energies in that area of the body were redirected.

What are we to make of such claims? Is it okay to utilize New Age techniques in search of miraculous cures? As we will see in what follows, I believe there is great danger in utilizing such New Age health techniques.

Most people in our society are utterly unaware of any such dangers and have felt free to dabble in this new form of medical treatment. It might surprise you to learn that New Age medicine is now a $27-billion-a-year industry, according to *Time* magazine. The magazine noted that 30 percent of the people it polled had tried an unconventional New Age therapy.[1] In fact, over 61 million Americans have tried a New Age therapy in just one single year.[2]

My big concern is that many people—*even Christians*—have been introduced to a New Age worldview by being treated with a "holistic" health therapy. It is alarming to note a poll's finding that a significant percentage of Christians (23 percent of Protestants and 59 percent of Catholics) believe New Age medical practices are compatible with Christianity.[3]

New Age Energetic Medicine

As you might have gathered from the story I told above, the New Age model of holistic health is heavily based on the concept of energy, not matter. The editors of the *New Age Journal* report:

> All of the healing systems that can be called "holistic"
> share a common belief in the universe as a unified
> field of energy that produces all form and sub-
> stance....This vital force, which supports and sustains
> life, has been given many names. The Chinese call it
> "*chi'i*," the Hindus call it "*prana*," the Hebrews call it
> "*ruach*," and the American Indians name it "the Great
> Spirit."[4]

This energy is not a visible, measurable, scientifically
explainable energy. Rather, New Agers speak of a "cosmic"
or "universal" energy based on their monistic *(all is one)* and
pantheistic *(all is God)* worldview. To enhance the flow of
"healing energy" in the body, one must allegedly attune oneself to it and realize one's unity with all things. Becoming
"one" with this universal energy ("God") yields health. (After
all, whoever heard of a sick god?) One must also "smooth
out" any energy blockages that may develop within the body.
Then one will be healthy. Many New Age health therapies
are based on this premise.[5]

There are many New Age energetic health therapies I
could mention. Following are just a few of the more notable:

- *Therapeutic Touch.* The practitioner places his or her
  hands two or three inches above the patient's body,
  palms down, and moves the hands up and down the
  body in search of energy imbalances. What is actually
  "touched" is a person's "energy field" around the
  body. By using circular sweeping motions, the
  patient's blocked energy is "decongested." This
  allegedly yields health for the patient. The healer also
  seeks to transfer healing energy from him- or herself
  into the body of the patient. This transfer of energy is
  also believed to yield health.

- *Rolfing.* This therapy is also based on the assumption that sickness is caused by energy blockages in the body. Rolfing seeks to relieve such energy blockages by applying deep pressure or massage to the body. It has been described as "massage with a vengeance."

- *Acupuncture/Acupressure.* Both of these therapies seek to unblock and redirect energy flow in the body using either needles or pressure points at strategic points in the body.

- *Chiropractic.* Some chiropractors are New Agers. In their treatments they typically combine spinal adjustments with some form of "energy balancing" to treat various bodily ailments.[6] Other chiropractors are *not* New Agers. They do not subscribe to the New Age worldview (they disavow any use of "energy balancing"[7]) and simply use chiropractic as a method to treat neuromusculoskeletal disorders (such as backaches).

These and a number of other New Age health therapies have served to introduce millions of Americans to a New Age belief system. New Age medicine, with its heavy emphasis on energy balancing, is truly a gateway into the New Age.

Energetic Medicine and the Power of the Mind

There are many New Agers today who believe that a key to controlling the energy in the body is the proper use of the mind. Best-selling New Age authors who subscribe to this view include Andrew Weil, Bernie Siegel, and Deepak Chopra.

Of course, there is more to the medical theories of Weil, Siegel, and Chopra than "energetic medicine." For my present purposes, however, I am limiting my attention to the worldview behind energetic medicine because this aspect of the New Age movement has made definite inroads into the Christian church—and thus there is need for discernment in this area.

Andrew Weil and Energy Centers (Chakras)

In his book *Spontaneous Healing,* Andrew Weil encourages readers to think of their bodies as energy.[8] He also expresses belief in *chakras*—seven centers of spiritual energy, according to yoga philosophy, that are situated in the "subtle" body that permeates the physical body.

In his book *Natural Health, Natural Medicine,* Weil talks about energy blockages within the body and how they relate to physical symptoms. Below is a quotation from Weil's book. But be forewarned: Unless you've already done study in this area, it may not make much sense to you. I provide this excerpt only to illustrate what millions of people in our society are buying into:

> In yoga physiology the heart region is one of the seven great centers (chakras) that organize the flow of energy around the body. The fourth, or heart, chakra participates in emotional connections to other people and the world beyond the self. Since the three lower chakras have to do with survival, sex, and power, the heart chakra is the first of the centers concerned with "higher" matters, with altruism, for example, and with love. If energy is blocked at this level through failure to open the heart, it cannot reach and activate the fifth, sixth, and seventh chakras, which control higher spiritual development. In this sense, blocked hearts and heart attacks mirror our emotional life and our ability to manage our feelings.[9]

Yikes! What was *that* all about? Weil's "bottom line" to keep in mind is simply that if the energy in the body gets "blocked" somewhere, you will develop physical symptoms. To maintain health, *you must keep that energy unblocked.*

Bernie Siegel's "Energetic" God

In his bestselling book *Peace, Love and Healing,* Bernie Siegel describes God as an "intelligent, loving energy."[10] In his second book, *Love, Medicine and Miracles,* he says, "I think of God as the same potential healing force—an intelligent, loving energy or light—in each person's life."[11] Siegel affirms that

> the "spiritual life" has many meanings. It need not be reflected in any commitment to an organized religion....I view the force behind creation as a loving, intelligent energy. For some, this is labeled God, for others it can be seen simply as a source of healing.[12]

Siegel also believes human beings are simply manifestations of this divine energy:

> Just as I believe that love and laughter and peace of mind are physiological, so I also believe that in our earthly lives we exist as physical manifestations of the loving, intelligent energy that we call God, the wholeness of the individual is the wholeness of the universe in microcosm. Atomically, anatomically, and cosmically we express this unity whether or not we are conscious of it.[13]

Siegel's view of the afterlife is an outgrowth of his view that God is an energy and that we are manifestations of that energy. "From my experience I feel that we do live on in some other form of energy after the body dies. I don't just say this to make people feel better, but because I have seen and heard about such extraordinary events."[14] Siegel has told stories of patients who have had departed loved ones appear to them in different visible forms.[15]

In an interview published in *New Age Journal,* Siegel commented,

> If you say to me, do I believe we live on in some other kind of energy after the body dies, yes. I mean, there are just too many interesting things I see happening in terms of communication to me from people who have died. So I am intrigued. But whether it goes to heaven or just goes back to the original source of energy that created the universe, if you want to call it God—I mean, you are just playing games with words—what's the difference? And can that energy pick out a new body? I don't know. I mean, what difference does it make?[16]

Deepak Chopra on Prana

In a *Time* magazine report on Deepak Chopra's medical views, we are told that understanding the universal energy, and our relationship to it, is the key to attaining and maintaining health:

> Our bodies, which seem so solid and finite, are not. For one thing, we replace most of our component cells regularly; thus, rather than collections of aging organs, we are works in constant progress. On the subatomic level, moreover, we are no denser than the air around us and indistinguishable from our surroundings. Finally, since quantum physics asserts that matter and energy are interchangeable, we are not individual beings at all but merely local expressions of an infinite, universal field of energy. A *smart* field of energy: "All of us are connected to patterns of intelligence

that govern the whole cosmos. Our bodies are part of a universal body, our minds an aspect of a universal mind."[17]

In his book *Ageless Body, Timeless Mind,* Chopra cites what he considers to be proof that we are all a part of this universal field of energy:

> Because your body emanates electromagnetic frequencies, you are yet another expression of the same [universal] field. The pulsations of nerve signals racing along your limbs, the electric charge emitted by your heart cells, and the faint field of current surrounding your brain all demonstrate that you are not separate from any form of energy in the universe. Any appearance of separation is only the product of the limitation of your senses, which are not attuned to these energies.[18]

Chopra often describes his views on universal energy with the term *prana.* He explains it this way:

> Prana is present in every mental and physical event; it flows directly from spirit, or pure awareness, to bring intelligence and consciousness to every aspect of life. You sometimes see Prana defined as "life force" or "life energy," but what is more important than a definition is to get experiential knowledge of it. If you can experience Prana, you can begin to nurture and preserve it. The critical importance of life energy has been recognized in many cultural traditions; the Chinese know it as *chi* and control its flow through acupuncture, meditation, and specialized exercises such as Tai Chi. Other names for the breath of life appear in Sufism, mystic Christianity, and the teachings of ancient Egypt. What is universally agreed on is that the more Prana you have, the more vital your mental and bodily processes.[19]

Understanding prana and how to manipulate it is said to bring health to the body. Prana, according to Chopra, "can be increased and decreased at will, moved here and there, and manipulated to keep the physical body orderly and young....The ability to contact and use Prana is within all of us."[20]

Chopra notes that "when Prana is kept from flowing... pockets of inertia and stagnation develop, eventually promoting disease. Depression is a state of almost complete nonflow and is associated with chronic illness, premature aging, and early death."[21]

This is where the power of the mind comes into the picture, because consciousness is said to be able to control this invisible energy. Indeed, because the body is viewed as nothing other than the projection of our own consciousness, an "unhealthy" or "unenlightened" consciousness will necessarily cause disease in the body. Therefore it is not surprising that consciousness, which supposedly regulates this invisible process, is the true "healer" in Chopra's system of thought.[22] He views meditation as the most important tool of the mind.[23]

We must not forget, Chopra tells us, that "the mind and body are inseparably one,"[24] and that "the mind exerts the deepest influence on the body."[25] He says "our cells are constantly eavesdropping on our thoughts and being changed by them."[26] Indeed, "the mind can go deep enough to change the very patterns that design the body. It can wipe mistakes off the blueprint, so to speak, and destroy any disease—cancer, diabetes, coronary heart disease—that has disturbed the design."[27] In fact, "because the mind influences every cell in the body, human aging is fluid and changeable. It can speed up, slow down, stop for a time and even reverse itself."[28]

The human body, Chopra says, "is a product of awareness."[29] "The world you live in, including the experience of your body, is completely dictated by how you learned to perceive it. If you change your perception, you change the experience of your body and your world."[30] "Impulses of intelligence create your body in new forms every second. What you are is the sum total of these impulses, and by changing their patterns, you will change."[31] What all this boils down to is that by learning to use your mind rightly through meditation, you can manipulate prana and bring health to your body.

Warning: Energetic Medicine May Be Hazardous to Your Spiritual Health

As I pondered what I had read in these books by Chopra, Weil, Siegel, and other New Agers, a number of thoughts came to mind. For example, if we are really a part of the divine (as Siegel indicates), why is it necessary for us to buy books from New Agers in order to find out about it? (If we were God, *wouldn't we already know it?*) And if all is truly "one" in the universe, as New Agers argue, then how is it possible for sickness and health to coexist in the first place? Further, if we are already a part of the divine, then how can we *get* sick? (Can *any* part of God get sick?) There seem to be numerous logical inconsistencies in the worldview the New Age health gurus are trying to sell us. These facts alone ought to make one highly suspicious about New Age energetic medicine.

It is my belief that no Christian should condone (or get involved in) any kind of a health model that is rooted in spiritual deception and that will likely compromise his or her commitment to Christ and Christianity. As Christian apologist Douglas Groothuis once put it,

> Whatever the efficacy of these various practices, the Christian must be careful to test the spirits to uncover

unbiblical ideas (1 John 4:1). Christians realize that the spiritual realm is real but not uniformly benevolent. A host of rebellious spirits or demons can masquerade as agents of healing and health for the purpose of diverting attention from the Great Physician.[32]

As one examines the specifics of energetic medicine, along with the various psychotechnologies (mind-altering techniques) that go along with it, numerous concerns emerge that cause the discerning Christian to do an about-face. In what follows I will summarize just a few basic concerns.

Different Concepts of God

Does it bother anyone that all of the major New Age health gurus are open to all kinds of different concepts of God? Weil's words confirm this: "I do not think it matters much how you conceive of that higher power; what matters is the sense of connection to it. It can be the father-god of the Old Testament, Jesus Christ, the Compassionate Buddha, the Great Spirit, the Goddess, pure, undifferentiated Consciousness, or simply the Mystery."[33] *Any ol' God will do just fine!*

Siegel, too, is open to all kinds of different religious belief systems. Any will do just fine! In an interview recorded in *New Age Journal,* Siegel said:

> The nicest compliment I get is people coming up and saying, "Just what religion are you?" I was brought up in the Jewish religion. Last night [when I spoke to a group] the minister thought I was Catholic, and I said, "Thank you, that's a wonderful compliment." Because, if they can't tell [my religion, it supports] the point I am making: Spirituality is universal. Religions are a problem, but spirituality and love are not.[34]

The Occult Connection

There is an undeniable and very strong connection between energetic medicine and occultism. Indeed, New Age critic Elliot Miller points out:

> Wherever it has appeared—in ancient paganism, modern occultism, or parapsychological research—this "life force" has been accompanied by altered states of consciousness, psychic phenomena, and contact with spirits. Additionally, those who are capable of perceiving and adept at manipulating this force invariably are shamans (for example, witch doctors), "sensitives," or psychics, thoroughly immersed in the pagan/occult world.[35]

Many holistic health therapies seek to enhance the flow of "healing energy" in the body. Unfortunately, by engaging in such holistic practices, many people have been pulled headlong into New Age occultism. Indeed, as Miller puts it, "My wide-ranging research of occultism emboldens me to suggest that this energy is part and parcel of the occult—where the occult appears, it can be found; where it is found, the occult will inevitably appear."[36]

This claim is verified in examining the writings of Chopra, Siegel, Weil, and other New Agers. For example, consider the following excerpt from *Love, Medicine and Miracles* in which Bernie Siegel speaks of how he met his spirit guide:

> The Simontons taught us how to meditate. At one point they led us in a directed meditation to find and meet an inner guide. I approached this exercise with all the skepticism one expects from a mechanistic doctor. Still, I sat down, closed my eyes, and followed directions. I didn't believe it would work, but if it did

I expected to see Jesus or Moses. Who else would dare appear inside a surgeon's head?

Instead I met George, a bearded, long-haired young man wearing an immaculate flowing white gown and a skullcap. It was an incredible awakening for me, because I hadn't expected anything to happen. As the Simontons taught us to communicate with whomever we'd called up from our unconscious minds, I found that talking to George was like playing chess with myself, but without knowing what my alter ego's next move would be.

George was spontaneous, aware of my feelings, and an excellent adviser....All I know is that he has been my invaluable companion ever since his first appearance. My life is much easier now, because he does the hard work.[37]

This is sheer occultism! Yet it is couched in such seemingly benign and innocuous language, it sounds as though what Siegel encountered should be a part of all our experiences.

During his trip to South America, Asia, and India, Andrew Weil admits to having worked with shamans and faith healers.[38] In his book *Natural Health, Natural Medicine,* he expresses openness to Zen meditation and the use of mantras.[39] These are distinctly unchristian practices that can lead one straight into the occult.

Christian apologists John Weldon and John Ankerberg have rightly noted that "almost all meditation other than biblical meditation develops psychic powers, inculcates a nonbiblical, occult worldview, and can open the door to spirit contact."[40] This is what happened to Siegel. This is what can happen to anyone who engages in the type of meditation espoused by Siegel, Weil, and Chopra.

The practice of visualization can also lead one straight into the occult:

> The number of well-meaning people who have
> embarked on a visualization program for physical
> health, psychological understanding, or spiritual
> advancement and ended up involved in the occult is
> not small. Books on visualization carry numerous
> anecdotes of how even the well-intentioned and seem-
> ingly nonoccult use of visualization catapulted people
> into the New Age movement, psychic development,
> and/or spirit contact.[41]

The attempt to control external reality by the mind is
an occultic practice and is hence totally off-limits for the
Christian. One must also recognize that man's imagination has been marred and infected by sin (Genesis 6:5).
Hence, visualization involves the use of faulty and untrustworthy equipment. How much better it is to trust in an
omniscient and omnipotent God than in one's visualizing
prowess!

How should the Christian view New Age energetic
medicine? In answering this question, I must point out
that if this energy is inherently occultic (and thus
demonic), as I have argued, then Christians involved with
it may become confused and compromised. One might
end up being drawn further into occultic practices. One's
Christian faith and life might deteriorate severely. This is
not a mere theoretical possibility, but has in fact happened
in the past.[42]

Scripture warns us of the pervasive influence of Satan
in this present world system. Indeed, "the whole world lies
in the power of the evil one" (1 John 5:19). This being the
case, the fact that millions of Americans are participating
in New Age energetic health practices—thereby intro-
ducing millions to the world of occultism—is not surprising.

We should beware! Indeed, as Groothuis puts it:

Much of what purports to be holistic is often less than holy; it may result in the horrors of occult oppression. In disguising himself as an angel of light (2 Corinthians 11:14), Satan may hide his poisonous intent under the white robes of the mystic healer. But the poison remains.[43]

Healing Is Ultimately God's Choice

As this book has argued, we as Christians most definitely believe in miraculous healing, but we also believe that healing is the *choice of a sovereign God who rules the universe*— a God who is separate and distinct from finite man (see Numbers 23:19; Ecclesiastes 5:2; Isaiah 45:18). God may *or may not* sovereignly choose to miraculously heal a person on any given occasion. The choice is entirely *His*, based on *His* will and power and not the choice of finite man.[44]

For the record, the scriptural perspective is this: As a result of the entrance of sin into the world, our physical bodies are continuously *running down* and suffering various ailments (contrary to Chopra's goal of an "ageless body"). Our present bodies are said to be perishable and weak (1 Corinthians 15:42-44). Paul said "our outer man is decaying" (2 Corinthians 4:16 NASB). Death and disease will be a part of the human condition until that time when we receive resurrection bodies that are immune to such frailties (1 Corinthians 15:51-55).

So, again, even though it is good and right to seek miraculous healing for our illnesses, we must submit our desires to the sovereign will of God. But even if we don't get healed in this life, we as Christians have a wonderful future to look forward to. Our hope comes in the Redeemer, whose work at the cross guarantees that all who believe in Him will not only live with Him forever, but will do so in perfect bodies that will never decay, grow old, or die.

Points to Ponder

- New Age health gurus hold to unbiblical views of God (that is, "all is God" and "you are god").

- This means that any "miracles" New Age health gurus claim to result from their techniques cannot be of the one true God (see Deuteronomy 13:1-3).

- New Age health techniques are rooted in occultism, and God forbids all contact with occultism (Deuteronomy 18:10-12). Hence, these techniques should be avoided.

- Any miraculous healing technique based on "balancing energy" in the body is not of God. Avoid it.

~

FOURTEEN

If Your Miracle Doesn't Come...

Trusting God *no matter what the circumstances* is one of the most important lessons God desires us to learn during our short time on earth. He often governs the circumstances of our lives in such a way that we are forced to see the importance of this lesson.

If that miraculous intervention from God you've been praying for doesn't materialize, *do not conclude that God has forgotten you.* For some special reason that you don't know right now, God has chosen to allow you to continue to go through what you're going through. Rest in Him and trust that He knows best. You may not be able to see Him or His host of angels, but there is an invisible world all around you—and the God of all comfort will never leave you alone in your suffering (2 Corinthians 1:3,4). Have faith. *He is with you even now.*

The apostle Paul defines faith as "being sure of what we hope for and certain of what we do not see" (Hebrews 11:1). I like John Wesley's paraphrase of this verse: "Faith is the power to see into the world of spirits, into things invisible and eternal. It is the power to understand those things which are not perceived by worldly senses."[1]

Of course, the big problem for most of us is that we tend to base everything on what our five senses tell us. And since the spiritual world is not subject to any of these, our faith is often weak and impotent.

Devotional writer A. W. Tozer pictures the problem this way:

> The world of sense intrudes upon our attention day and night for the whole of our lifetime. It is clamorous, insistent, and self-demonstrating. It does not appeal to our faith; it is here, assaulting our five senses, demanding to be accepted as real and final. But sin has so clouded the lenses of our hearts that we cannot see that other reality, the City of God, shining around us. The world of sense triumphs.[2]

The eye of faith, however, perceives this unseen reality. The spiritual world lies all about us, enclosing us, embracing us, altogether within our reach. God Himself is here awaiting our response to His presence. He is here to comfort us. This spiritual world will come alive to us the moment we begin to reckon upon its reality.

Do you remember the story of Elisha in 2 Kings 6:8-23? Elisha found himself in a situation where he was completely surrounded by enemy troops, yet he remained calm and relaxed. His servant, however, must have been shaking in his boots at the sight of this hostile army with vicious-looking warriors and innumerable battle-chariots on every side.

Undaunted, Elisha said to him: "Don't be afraid. ...Those who are with us are more than those who are with them" (2 Kings 6:16). Elisha then prayed to God, " 'O LORD, open his eyes so he may see.' Then the LORD opened the servant's eyes, and he looked and saw the hills full of horses and chariots of fire all around Elisha" (2 Kings 6:17). God was protecting Elisha and his servant with a whole army of magnificent angelic beings!

The reason Elisha never got worried was because he was sure of what he hoped for and certain of what he did not see (Hebrews 11:1). The eye of faith recognizes that God acts on our behalf even when we don't perceive it with our physical senses. So, again, if a miracle has not come your way, *do not fret.* The invisible but almighty God is with you. No matter what you go through, He is there right beside you. You are never alone!

Conditioning the "Faith Muscle"

I've always been taught that faith is like a muscle. A muscle has to be repeatedly stretched to its limit of endurance in order to build more strength. Without increased stress in training, the muscle will simply not grow.

In the same way, faith must be repeatedly tested to the limit of its endurance in order to expand and develop. Very often, God allows His children to go through trying experiences in order to develop their "faith muscles." Sometimes God may delay sending that miracle we think we need for this very reason.

This principle is beautifully illustrated in the book of Exodus. Following Israel's deliverance from Egypt, God first led them to Marah, a place where they would have to trust God to heal the water to make it drinkable. It is significant that God led them to Marah before leading them to Elim, a gorgeous oasis with plenty of good water (Exodus 15:22-27). God could have bypassed Marah altogether and brought them directly to Elim if He had wanted to. But, as is characteristic of God, He purposefully led them through the route that would yield maximum conditioning of their faith muscles.

God does the same type of thing with us. He often governs our circumstances so as to yield maximum conditioning of our faith muscles. If you find yourself in a difficult situation right now, it could be that God has purposefully brought you to this point in order to stretch your faith muscles.

Faith and the Word of God

John Calvin once said "we must be reminded that there is a permanent relationship between faith and the Word. God could not separate one from the other any more than we could separate the rays from the sun from which they come."[3] Indeed, God's Word "is the basis whereby faith is supported and sustained; if it turns away from the Word, it falls. Therefore, take away the Word and no faith will then remain."[4]

The New Testament writers were adamant on this issue. John's Gospel tells us "these [things] are written that you may believe" (John 20:31). Paul tells us "faith comes from hearing the message, and the message is heard through the word of Christ" (Romans 10:17). If someone should ask, "How can I increase my faith?" the answer is: *Saturate your mind with God's Word.* What this means on a day-to-day level is that if your much-needed miracle has not come, you can be sustained by the faith that results from drinking richly of God's Word. *Do not neglect daily feasting upon Scripture.*

Here are two very important pieces of advice on faith from a modern-day faith warrior:

- First, since true faith is solidly anchored upon scriptural facts, we must not allow ourselves to be influenced by mere emotional impressions. "Impressions have neither one thing nor the other to do with faith," says George Müller. "Faith has to do with the Word of God. It is not impressions, strong or weak, which will make the difference. We have to do with the written Word and not ourselves or impressions."[5]

- Second, we must beware of letting probabilities hinder our faith. Again, it is Müller who warns: "Many people are willing to believe regarding those things that seem probable to them. Faith has nothing to do with probabilities. The province of faith begins where probabilities cease and sight and sense fail. Appearances are not to be taken into account."[6]

So—trust God *no matter how bad things appear.* God is in control. Rest securely in His sovereign direction of your life's affairs.

Never Stop Praying

One passage I always keep in mind when times are tough is Matthew 7:7,8, in which Jesus said, "Ask and it will be given to you; seek and you will find; knock and the door will be opened to you. For everyone who asks receives; he who seeks finds; and to him who knocks, the door will be opened."

The tenses in the Greek for this verse actually carry the idea, "*Keep on* asking and it will be given; *keep on* seeking and you will find; *keep on* knocking and the door will be opened." This verse explicitly tells us not to give up on prayer. We need to hang in there. We need to maintain faith.

The reason I bring this up is that sometimes Christians get discouraged if they don't get an immediate answer to prayer. Also, some Christians think that if they ask for the same thing more than one time in prayer, they must have originally asked without faith. But this is not the teaching of Scripture. We are to *keep on* asking, *keep on* seeking, *keep on* knocking. Never give up on prayer. Never lose faith.

Though space prohibits a detailed treatment of prayer in this chapter, there are a few brief pointers I want to mention that have greatly helped me through the years. These are especially important:

- We must remember that all our prayers are subject to the sovereign will of God. If we ask for something God doesn't want us to have, He will sovereignly deny that request. First John 5:14 instructs us, "This is the confidence we have in approaching God: that if we ask anything *according to his will*, he hears us" (emphasis added).

- Prayer should not be an occasional practice but rather a continual practice. We are instructed in 1 Thessalonians 5:17 to "*pray continually.*" It should be a daily habit.

- Recognize that sin is a hindrance to prayer being answered. Psalm 66:18 says, "If I had cherished sin in my heart, the Lord would not have listened."

- Living righteously, on the other hand, is a great benefit to prayer being answered. Proverbs 15:29 says, "The LORD is far from the wicked but he hears the prayer of the righteous."

- A good model prayer is the Lord's Prayer found in Matthew 6:9-13. Within this one single prayer we find praise (verse 9), personal requests (verses 11-13), and an affirmation of God's will (verse 10).

- If your prayer seems unanswered, keep trusting God *no matter what*. He has a reason for the delay. You can count on it.

Looking Toward Eternity

God's occasional blessing of miracles and His providential answers to prayer bring much consolation to us during our earthly sojourn as we make our way to the heavenly city (Hebrews 11:16). We may rightly rejoice over the fact that God does indeed answer our prayers, and that He often comes through for us in ways that we never could have expected. However, *we must never let our desire for miracles come between us and God.*

We are not to look to miraculous phenomena in themselves for our refuge. *God* is our refuge, and we are to invoke *His* aid—and at *His* prerogative, He may or *may not* choose to miraculously intervene in whatever situation we find ourselves in. He knows best. And we must submit to His infinitely wise understanding. *He* is the object of our faith, not the miracles. As Adrian Rogers put it, we must "learn to believe in miracles, but to trust in Jesus."[7]

As we continue to keep Christ supreme in our hearts, we can contemplate the greatness of what lies ahead. As Scripture tells us, "No eye has seen, no ear has heard, no mind has conceived what God has prepared for those who love him" (1 Corinthians 2:9). Pondering this wonderful future reality can put "wind in our sails" during those times when life throws us a punch and that much-desired miracle seems to elude us.

Reflect on how the apostle John describes our eternal destiny:

> Then I saw a new heaven and a new earth, for the first heaven and the first earth had passed away, and there was no longer any sea. I saw the Holy City, the new Jerusalem, coming down out of heaven from God, prepared as a bride beautifully dressed for her husband. And I heard a loud voice from the throne saying, "Now the dwelling of God is with men, and he will live with them. They will be his people, and God himself will be with them and be their God. He will wipe every tear from their eyes. There will be no more

death or mourning or crying or pain, for the old order of things has passed away."

He who was seated on the throne said, "I am making everything new!" Then he said, "Write this down, for these words are trustworthy and true" (Revelation 21:1-5).

The incredible glory of the afterlife—our real life—should motivate each of us to live faithfully during our relatively short time on earth. Especially when difficult times come, we must remember that we are only pilgrims on our way to another land—to the undiscovered country, the final frontier of heaven where God Himself dwells.

J. I. Packer once said that the "lack of long, strong thinking about our promised hope of glory is a major cause of our plodding, lackluster lifestyle."[8] Packer points to the Puritans as a much-needed example for us, for they believed that "it is the heavenly Christian that is the lively Christian."[9] The Puritans understood that we "run so slowly, and strive so lazily, because we so little mind the prize....So let Christians animate themselves daily to run the race set before them by practicing heavenly meditation."[10]

I have come to appreciate the Puritans, and I personally seek to imitate their example! The Puritans "saw themselves as God's pilgrims, traveling home through rough country; God's warriors, battling the world, the flesh, and the devil; and God's servants, under orders to worship, fellowship, and do all the good they could as they went along."[11] We should all have this attitude.

I am particularly impressed with the writings of the Puritan Richard Baxter. Truly he had some habits worthy of imitation. His first habit was to "estimate everything—values, priorities, possessions, relationships, claims, tasks—as these things will appear when one actually comes to die."[12] In other words, he weighed everything in terms of eternal benefit. After all, our life on earth is short; our life in heaven is forever. If we work only for the things of this earth, what eternal benefit will all of it have?

Baxter's second habit was to "dwell on the glory of the heavenly life to which one was going."[13] Baxter daily practiced "holding heaven at the forefront of his thoughts and desires."[14] The hope of heaven brought him joy, and joy brought him strength. Baxter once said, "A heavenly mind is a joyful mind; this is the nearest and truest way to live a life of comfort....A heart in heaven will be a most excellent preservative against temptations, a powerful means to kill thy corruptions."[15]

Christian apologists Gary R. Habermas and J. P. Moreland have come up with a term I like a lot: *a "top-down" perspective.* That's precisely what we need during our earthly pilgrimage as we journey toward our heavenly destiny:

> The God of the universe invites us to view life and death from his eternal vantage point. And if we do, we will see how readily it can revolutionize our lives: daily anxieties, emotional hurts, tragedies, our responses and responsibilities to others, possessions, wealth, and even physical pain and death. All of this and much more can be informed and influenced by the truths of heaven. The repeated witness of the New Testament is that believers should view all problems, indeed, their entire existence, from what we call the "top-down" perspective: God and his kingdom first, followed by various aspects of our earthly existence.[16]

A key passage on the "top-down" perspective is Matthew 6:19-34. Here Jesus informs us that anxiety will not change anything. Certainly it will not increase the length of our lives (see verse 27). Our goal therefore should be to store up treasures in heaven. This will help rid our lives of anxiety. Make note of this principle: *The position of our hearts will coincide with the placement of our treasures.*

If we are usually anxious over temporal problems, our hearts are not centered on what should properly be our first love. If we have perpetual anxiety, we are more occupied with transient realities than Jesus intended. So here we have a ready-made test by which we can assess the depth of our beliefs.[17]

Our goal, then, should be to maintain a "top-down" perspective. This perspective is a radical love of God that places Him first and foremost in every aspect of our lives. "Set your minds on things above, not on earthly things" (Colossians 3:2). And when we do this, God has promised to meet all our earthly needs as part of the package (Matthew 6:33)!

Hope that Fuels Faith

Our *hope* in the future glory of the afterlife fuels our *faith* during the present. *Hope* and *faith*—these are closely tied to each other in the pages of Scripture. The apostle Paul tells us faith involves "being sure of what we *hope* for" (Hebrews 11:1).

In his classic *Institutes of the Christian Religion,* John Calvin delineates for us hope's relation to faith:

> Hope refreshes faith, that it may not become weary. It sustains faith to the final goal, that it may not fail in midcourse, or even at the starting gate. In short, by unremitting renewing and restoring, it invigorates faith again and again with perseverance.[18]

One of my favorite Old Testament characters is Moses. His life vividly illustrates how hope can feed and sustain faith:

> *By faith* Moses, when he had grown up, refused to be known as the son of Pharaoh's daughter. He chose to be mistreated along with the people of God rather

> than to enjoy the pleasures of sin for a short time. He
> regarded disgrace for the sake of Christ as of greater
> value than the treasures of Egypt, *because he was looking
> ahead to his reward. By faith* he left Egypt, not fearing
> the king's anger; he persevered because *he saw him
> who is invisible* (Hebrews 11:24-27, emphasis added).

Moses could have had immeasurable power, authority, and riches if he had chosen to stay in Egypt. Yet he gave it all up because of his faith in God. He perceived another King, another kingdom. And his faith was nourished by his *hope* of a future reward, a hope of living in the eternal city with the living Lord of the universe, a hope that gave him an *eternal* perspective.

Truly our faith enables us to perceive the eternal. As John Wesley put it,

> True Christian faith fulfills man's desires to perceive
> the eternal. It gives him a more extensive knowledge
> of all things invisible. Living faith introduces him to
> what the eye has not seen, nor the ear heard, nor the
> heart conceived in the clearest light, with the fullest
> certainty and evidence. Knowing these benefits, who
> would not wish for such a faith? With faith comes not
> only this awareness, but also the fulfillment of the
> promise of holiness and happiness.[19]

Walking by sight causes us to behold disease, decay, and death as regular features of our world. But walking by faith enables us to see the reality beyond the physical senses to see into the world of the eternal. And the destiny of those who believe in Jesus Christ is a wonderful destiny indeed. For we will live forever with Christ in resurrected bodies that will never again be susceptible to disease, decay, and death. *Let our faith cause us to rejoice in this!*

The great preacher Charles Spurgeon once said, "A little faith will bring your soul to heaven; a great faith will bring heaven to your soul."[20] One of the ways faith brings heaven to our souls is in our realization of our heavenly destiny with Christ. Such faith rests in the assurance that regardless of what happens on this puny speck of a planet, our destiny is the eternal city, the heavenly country, to be at the very side of Christ.

So again, if you feel your miracle has not come, *do not fret*. Rest with the assurance God is in control and He has a purpose for allowing your present circumstances. Saturate your heart with the Word of God, and let that saturation fan your faith and your hope into a flame. Know that God is with you. You are not alone. Rest in Him, and let the joy of the Lord be your strength!

APPENDIX

~

The Miracle of a Changed Life

Many Christians throughout church history have made note of the miraculous element that is involved in a fallen sinner converting to Christ:

- Baptist preacher Adrian Rogers said that "the greatest miracle is the transformation that God works when he regenerates a soul."[1]

- Writer Philip James Bailey said, "Every believer is God's miracle."[2]

- Martin Luther once wrote: "Conversion is the greatest of all miracles. Every day witnesses miracle after miracle; that any village adheres to the Gospel when a hundred thousand devils are arrayed against it, or that the truth is maintained in this wicked world, is a continued miracle to which healing the sick or raising the dead is a mere trifle."[3]

- Leonard Ravenhill said that "the greatest miracle that God can do today is to take an unholy man out of an unholy world, and make that man holy and put him back into that unholy world and keep him holy in it."[4]

- Creationist Henry Morris wrote: "The miracle of regeneration is a grade A miracle in every sense of the word. A person who is a *closed system* spiritually, utterly inadequate and self-centered, suddenly becomes an *open system* integrated and with his life centered in the omnipotent Creator. He who was spiritually deteriorating day after day—as a matter of fact, already 'dead while he liveth'—suddenly experiences 'peace and joy in believing, through the power of the Holy Ghost' (Romans 15:13) and becomes 'quickened together with Christ' (Ephesians 2:5)."[5]

Those of us who remember what our lives were like before converting to Christ can readily testify to the miraculous way God has worked in our individual lives! *Praise God for the miracle of the new birth!*

Bibliography

Berndt, Jodie. *Celebration of Miracles*. Nashville, Tennessee: Thomas Nelson Publishers, 1995.

The Bible Knowledge Commentary: New Testament. Edited by John F. Walvoord and Roy B. Zuck. Wheaton, Illinois: Victor Books, 1983.

The Bible Knowledge Commentary: Old Testament. Edited by John F. Walvoord and Roy B. Zuck. Wheaton, Illinois: Victor Books, 1985.

The Concise Evangelical Dictionary of Theology. Edited by Walter A. Elwell. Grand Rapids, Michigan: Baker Book House, 1991.

Geisler, Norman, and Ronald Brooks. *When Skeptics Ask*. Wheaton, Illinois: Victor Books, 1990.

Geisler, Norman, and Thomas Howe. *When Critics Ask: A Popular Handbook on Bible Difficulties*. Wheaton, Illinois: Victor Books, 1992.

Geisler, Norman, and Ron Rhodes. *When Cultists Ask*. Grand Rapids, Michigan: Baker Book House, 1997.

Ghezzi, Bert. *Miracles of the Saints: A Book of Reflections*. Grand Rapids, Michigan: Zondervan Publishing House, 1996.

Kreeft, Peter, and Ronald Tacelli. *Handbook of Christian Apologetics*. Downers Grove, Illinois: InterVarsity Press, 1994.

Lightner, Robert. *Evangelical Theology: A Survey and Review*. Grand Rapids, Michigan: Baker Book House, 1986.

————. *The God of the Bible*. Grand Rapids, Michigan: Baker Book House, 1978.

Mayhue, Richard. *The Healing Promise*. Eugene, Oregon: Harvest House Publishers, 1994.

McDowell, Josh. *The Resurrection Factor*. San Bernardino, California: Here's Life Publishers, 1981.

McDowell, Josh, and Don Stewart. *Answer to Tough Questions Skeptics Ask About the Christian Faith*. Wheaton, Illinois: Tyndale House Publishers, 1988.

————. *Reasons Skeptics Should Consider Christianity*. Wheaton, Illinois: Tyndale House Publishers, 1988.

Miracles Are Heaven Sent. Tulsa, Oklahoma: Honor Books, 1995.

Nelson's New Illustrated Bible Dictionary. Edited by Ronald Youngblood. Nashville, Tennessee: Thomas Nelson Publishers, 1995.

The NIV Study Bible. Edited by Kenneth Barker. Grand Rapids, Michigan: Zondervan Publishing House, 1985.

Rhodes, Ron. *Angels Among Us: Separating Truth from Fiction.* Eugene, Oregon: Harvest House Publishers, 1994.

————. *Christ Before the Manger: The Life and Times of the Preincarnate Christ.* Grand Rapids, Michigan: Baker Book House, 1992.

————. *The Counterfeit Christ of the New Age Movement.* Grand Rapids, Michigan: Baker Book House, 1990.

————. *The Culting of America: The Shocking Implications for Every Concerned Christian.* Eugene, Oregon: Harvest House Publishers, 1994.

————. *The Heart of Christianity: What It Means to Believe in Jesus.* Eugene, Oregon: Harvest House Publishers, 1996.

————. *Heaven: The Undiscovered Country—Exploring the Wonder of the Afterlife.* Eugene, Oregon: Harvest House Publishers, 1996.

————. *The New Age Movement.* Grand Rapids, Michigan: Zondervan Publishing House, 1995.

————. *Quick-Reference Guide to Angels.* Eugene, Oregon: Harvest House Publishers, 1997.

————. *When Servants Suffer: Finding Purpose in Pain.* Wheaton, Illinois: Harold Shaw Publishers, 1990.

Ryrie Study Bible. Edited by Charles Caldwell Ryrie. Chicago, Illinois: Moody Press, 1994.

Ryrie, Charles Caldwell. *Balancing the Christian Life.* Chicago, Illinois: Moody Press, 1969.

————. *Basic Theology.* Wheaton, Illinois: Victor Books, 1986.

————. *The Holy Spirit.* Chicago, Illinois: Moody Press, 1980.

————. *You Mean the Bible Teaches That...* Chicago, Illinois: Moody Press, 1974.

Sheridan, Tom. *Small Miracles: Extraordinary Stories of Ordinary People Touched By God.* Grand Rapids, Michigan: Zondervan Publishing House, 1996.

Sherrer, Quin. *Miracles Happen When You Pray.* Grand Rapids, Michigan: Zondervan Publishing House, 1997.

Story, Dan. *Defending Your Faith: How to Answer the Tough Questions.* Nashville, Tennessee: Thomas Nelson Publishers, 1992.

Walvoord, John F. *Jesus Christ Our Lord.* Chicago, Illinois: Moody Press, 1969.

Zondervan NIV Bible Commentary: New Testament. Edited by Kenneth L. Barker and John Kohlenberger III. Vol. 2. Grand Rapids, Michigan: Zondervan Publishing House, 1994.

Zondervan NIV Bible Commentary: Old Testament. Edited by Kenneth L. Barker and John Kohlenberger III. Vol. 1. Grand Rapids, Michigan: Zondervan Publishing House, 1994.

Notes

Chapter 1—When Heaven Touches Earth

1. This true event is recounted by Colin Whittaker, *Seven Guides to Effective Prayer* (Minneapolis, Minnesota: Bethany House Publishers, 1987), pp. 15-16. See also *The Autobiography of George Müller: The Life of Trust* (Grand Rapids, Michigan: Baker Book House, 1984).

2. Whittaker, p. 33. See *The Autobiography of George Müller: The Life of Trust.*

3. *Illustrations for Biblical Preaching,* Logos Bible Software, electronic media.

4. Elisabeth Elliot, *Shadow of the Almighty* (Grand Rapids, Michigan: Zondervan Publishing House, 1977), back cover.

5. Elliot, p. 199.

6. Elliot, p. 199.

7. Elliot, p. 199.

8. Fictitious names have been used to respect the privacy of the individuals involved.

9. Jodie Berndt, *Celebration of Miracles* (Nashville, Tennessee: Thomas Nelson Publishers, 1995), pp. 22-23.

10. Roger Steer, "Pushing Inward," *Christian History Magazine,* 1996, Issue 52, Vol. XV, No. 4, p. 10.

11. Steer, p. 10.

12. Whittaker, pp. 63-65.

13. Cited in Billy Graham, *Angels: God's Secret Agents* (New York, New York: Doubleday, 1975), p. 3.

14. Charles Swindoll, *The Finishing Touch* (Dallas, Texas: Word, Inc., 1994); cited in *Miracles Are Heaven Sent* (Tulsa, Oklahoma: Honor Books, 1995), p. 136.

15. Cited in *Bible Illustrations,* Parson's Technology, electronic media, insert added.

Chapter 2—The Popularity of Miracles

1. Deena Yellin, "Holiday of Miracles," *The Record,* December 3, 1999, p. 1.

2. "PAX TV to Launch 'America's Search for Miracles,' " 1999 Business Wire, Internet.

3. Ibid.

4. Ibid.

5. George Barna, Barna Research Online, 1994, http://www.barna.org.

6. Tom Sheridan, *Small Miracles: Extraordinary Stories of Ordinary People Touched by God* (Grand Rapids, Michigan: Zondervan Publishing House, 1996), p. 25.

7. Jodie Berndt, *Celebration of Miracles* (Nashville, Tennessee: Thomas Nelson Publishers, 1995), p. 2.

8. Sheridan, p. 27.

9. Sheridan, p. 27.

10. "Why More People Believe in God and Miracles," *Jet*, January 26, 1998, Gale Group Magazine, Johnson Publishing Company, p. 14, text downloaded from DIALOG database.

11. Margaret Carlin, "Heavenly Ideas," *Rocky Mountain News*, December 22, 1992, p. 49.

12. Claire Safran, "Do You Believe in Miracles?" *Redbook*, December 1993, p. 81, downloaded from DIALOG database.

13. Associated Press, "An Age for Angels," 1994, p. 4.

14. Yellin, p. 1.

15. "Why More People Believe in God and Miracles."

16. Sydney Ahlstrom, *A Religious History of the American People* (New York, New York: Image Books, 1975), p. 31.

17. Kenneth Boa, *Cults, World Religions, and You* (Wheaton, Illinois: Victor, 1979), p. 4.

18. Cited in Chuck Colson, *Against the Night* (Ann Arbor, Michigan: Servant Publications, 1989), p. 48.

19. Safran, p. 81.

20. Sheridan, pp. 30-31.

21. "Why More People Believe in God and Miracles."

22. "Why More People Believe in God and Miracles."

23. Philip Yancey, "Jesus, the Reluctant Miracle Worker," *Christianity Today*, May 19, 1997, p. 80.

Chapter 3—What Is a Miracle?

1. Philip Yancey, "Jesus, the Reluctant Miracle Worker," *Christianity Today*, May 19, 1997, p. 80.

2. Robert Dean, "The Myths of the Third Wave," *Biblical Perspectives*, Vol. 3, No. 4, July-August 1990, Biblical Awareness Ministries.

3. Wayne Grudem, *Systematic Theology* (Grand Rapids, Michigan: Zondervan Publishing House, 1995), electronic media, emphasis added.

4. Grudem.

5. Grudem.

6. Richard Purtill, in R. Douglas Geivett and Gary R. Habermas, *In Defense of Miracles: A Comprehensive Case for God's Action in History* (Downers Grove, Illinois: InterVarsity Press, 1997), p. 64.

7. J. I. Packer, *Concise Theology: A Guide to Historic Christian Beliefs* (Wheaton, Illinois: Tyndale House Publishers, no date), electronic media.

8. Jodie Berndt, *Celebration of Miracles* (Nashville, Tennessee: Thomas Nelson Publishers, 1995), p. 13.

9. C. S. Lewis, *Miracles* (New York, New York: Macmillan, 1960), p. 15.

10. J. Gresham Machen, *The Christian View of Man* (Banner of Truth, 1984), p. 117.

11. Packer.

12. *The New Unger's Bible Dictionary* (Chicago, Illinois: Moody Press, 1988), PC Study Bible, electronic media.

13. *Wycliffe Bible Encyclopedia* (Chicago, Illinois: Moody Press, no date), The Word Processor, electronic media.

14. Norman L. Geisler, *Encyclopedia of Apologetics* (Grand Rapids, Michigan: Baker Book House, 1999), p. 480.

15. *Thayer's Greek Lexicon*, QuickVerse Library, Broderbund, electronic media.

16. *Vine's Expository Dictionary of Biblical Words* (Nashville, Tennessee: Thomas Nelson Publishers, 1985), PC Study Bible, electronic media.

17. *The New Unger's Bible Dictionary*.

18. *Thayer's Greek Lexicon.*

19. *Vine's Expository Dictionary of Biblical Words.*

20. Richard Mayhue, *The Healing Promise* (Eugene, Oregon: Harvest House Publishers, 1994), p. 177.

21. Adrian Rogers, *Believe in Miracles but Trust in Jesus* (Wheaton, Illinois: Crossway Books, 1997), p. 12.

22. Josh McDowell and Don Stewart, *Answers to Tough Questions* (Nashville, Tennessee: Thomas Nelson Publishers, 1993), p. 80.

23. Spiros Zodhiates, *The Complete Word Study Dictionary: New Testament* (Chattanooga, Tennessee: AMG Publishers, 1992), p. 1286.

24. Packer.

25. *The New Unger's Bible Dictionary.*

26. *Easton's Dictionary, PC Study Bible,* electronic media.

27. Grudem.

28. Douglas Connelly, *Miracles: What the Bible Says* (Downers Grove, Illinois: InterVarsity Press, 1997), p. 18.

29. *The New Unger's Bible Dictionary.*

30. Charles C. Ryrie, *The Miracles of Our Lord* (Neptune, New Jersey: Loizeaux Brothers, 1988), p. 10.

31. Charles Hodge, *Systematic Theology,* Logos Bible Software, electronic media.

32. Henry Morris, "Biblical Naturalism and Modern Science," *Bibliotheca Sacra,* Logos Bible Software, electronic media.

33. Morris, "Biblical Naturalism and Modern Science."

34. Morris, "Biblical Naturalism and Modern Science."

35. R.C. Trench; quoted in Berndt, p. 128, insert mine.

36. Winfried Corduan, in Geivett and Habermas, pp. 104-105

37. Connelly, p. 20.

38. Morris.

39. Jackie Deere points out in regard to Jesus, the miracles testify to the following: "God is with Jesus (John 3:2); Jesus is from God (John 3:2; 9:32,33); God has sent Jesus (John 5:36); Jesus has authority on earth to forgive sins (Mark 2:10,11; Matthew 9:6,7; Luke 5:24,25); Jesus is approved by God (Acts 2:22); the Father is in Jesus and Jesus is in the Father (John 10:37,38; 14:11); in Jesus the kingdom of God has come (Matthew 12:28; Luke 11:20); and Jesus is the Messiah (Matthew 11:1-6; Luke 7:18-23) and the Son of God (Matthew 14:25-33)." (Jackie Deere, *Surprised by the Spirit* [Grand Rapids, Michigan: Zondervan Publishing House, 1993], p. 103.)

40. It seems prudent to note, however, that simply because an incredible miracle occurs does not guarantee that a *witness* to that miracle will become a believer in God or will commit himself or herself to deeper commitment to God. There is more than enough scriptural evidence that this simply is not the case.

    The Israelites are an excellent example. Though they had witnessed God's incredible miracles in the plagues that defeated Pharaoh and the Egyptians, they quickly degenerated into idolatry during the wilderness sojourn (see Exodus 32).

    We find examples in the New Testament as well. Amazingly, after Jesus performed the mighty miracle of feeding 5000 people, Scripture tells us: "From this time many of his disciples turned back and no longer followed him" (John 6:66).

41. Grudem.

Chapter 4—Miracles in the Old Testament

1. John J. Davis, *Moses and the Gods of Egypt: Studies in Exodus* (Grand Rapids, Michigan: Baker Book House, 1986), p. 94.

2. Davis, p. 97.

3. Davis, pp. 59, 81.

4. Davis, p. 100.

5. Pierre Montet, *Eternal Egypt* (New York, New York: The New American Library, 1964), p. 57.

6. Alan Cole, *Exodus: An Introduction and Commentary* (Downers Grove, Illinois: InterVarsity Press, 1973), p. 90.

7. *Ancient Near Eastern Texts*, edited by James B. Pritchard, "Hymn to the Nile," translated by John Wilson (Princeton, New Jersey: Princeton University Press, 1969), p. 272.

8. Old Testament scholar Merrill F. Unger tells us: "Moses appears in the OT as the first great miracle worker. And the reason for that is evident when we remember his unique position in the religious history of mankind, the greatness of his work, and the obstacles he encountered (Exodus 10:12; 14:21-31; 20:1-21; etc.)." (*The New Unger's Bible Dictionary*, "Miracles").

9. Norman L. Geisler, *A Popular Survey of the Old Testament* (Grand Rapids, Michigan: Baker Book House, 1977), p. 56.

10. Davis, p. 102.

11. Davis, p. 103.

12. Davis, p. 107.

13. Davis, p. 108.

14. Davis, p. 108.

15. C. F. Keil and F. Delitzsch, *The Pentateuch: Biblical Commentary on the Old Testament* (Grand Rapids, Michigan: Eerdmans Publishing Company, 1949), p. 483.

16. Montet, p. 177.

17. Cole, p. 93.

18. Davis, p. 114.

19. Geisler, p. 56.

20. Cole, p. 95.

21. See John B. Noss, *Man's Religions* (New York, New York: Macmillan Publishing Co., 1974), pp. 35-37.

22. Montet, p. 172.

23. Davis, pp. 122-23.

24. Cole, p. 96.

25. Davis, p. 123.

26. Davis, p. 124.

27. Geisler, p. 56.

28. Noss, p. 38.

29. Davis, p. 128.

30. Notice that some of the plagues — such as the plague of gnats, the hail, and the locusts — involved natural conditions that, in less extreme forms, have prevailed in the Nile valley from time to time. The miraculous element in these plagues is to be found in their timing *(when Moses said so)*, their intensity *(worse than ever)*, and the location (*in Egypt alone* and not in neighboring Goshen, where the Israelites were).

31. Davis, p. 130.

32. Montet, pp. 39,169.

33. C. J. Labuschagne, *The Incomparability of Yahweh in the Old Testament,* Pretoria Oriental Series (Leiden: Brill, 1966), p. 58.

34. Davis, p. 134.

35. *Ancient Near Eastern Texts,* pp. 367-68.

36. Davis, p. 134.

37. Davis, p. 141.

38. Davis, p. 149.

39. Geisler, p. 56

40. Davis, p. 149.

41. Cole, p. 92.

42. Labuschagne, p. 73.

Chapter 5—The Miracle of the Incarnation

1. John A. Witmer, "The Doctrine of Miracles," *Bibliotheca Sacra,* Logos Bible Software, electronic media.

2. Merrill Tenney, "Topics from the Gospel of John—Part III: The Meaning of 'Witness' in John," *Bibliotheca Sacra,* Logos Bible Software, electronic media.

3. Gene Getz, "The Christian Home — Part II," *Bibliotheca Sacra,* Logos Bible Software, electronic media.

4. Carl F. Henry, "What Is Christianity?" *Bibliotheca Sacra,* Logos Bible Software, electronic media.

5. Kenneth O. Gangel, "Moral Entropy, Creation, and the Battle for the Mind," *Bibliotheca Sacra,* Logos Bible Software, electronic media.

6. Erich Sauer, *The Triumph of the Crucified* (Grand Rapids, Michigan: Eerdmans Publishing Company, 1977), p. 13.

7. Robert G. Gromacki, *The Virgin Birth: Doctrine of Deity* (Grand Rapids, Michigan: Baker Book House, 1981), p. 101.

8. Gromacki, p. 102.

9. Gromacki, p. 103.

10. Edgar J. Goodspeed, *Modern Apocrypha* (Boston, Massachusetts: The Beacon Press, 1956), p. 7.

11. See Norman Geisler, *To Understand the Bible Look for Jesus* (Grand Rapids, Michigan: Baker Book House, 1979), p. 67.

12. John F. Walvoord, *Jesus Christ Our Lord* (Chicago, Illinois: Moody Press, 1980), p. 111.

13. See Millard Erickson, *Christian Theology* (Grand Rapids, Michigan: Baker Book House, 1987), p. 711.

14. Charles C. Ryrie, *Basic Theology* (Wheaton, Illinois: Victor Books, 1986), p. 261.

15. Benjamin Warfield, *The Person and Work of Christ* (Philadelphia, Pennsylvania: Presbyterian and Reformed Publishing Co., 1950), p. 39.

16. Warfield, p. 39.

17. Walvoord, p. 138.

18. Walvoord, pp. 138-39.

19. Robert L. Reymond, *Jesus, Divine Messiah: The New Testament Witness* (Phillipsburg, New Jersey: Presbyterian and Reformed Publishing Co., 1990), p. 258.

20. See Erickson, p. 734.

21. Walvoord, p. 141.

22. See also Geisler, p. 28.

23. Walvoord, p. 144.

24. Walvoord, p. 144.

25. Robert P. Lightner, "Philippians," in *The Bible Knowledge Commentary*, New Testament, eds. John F. Walvoord and Roy B. Zuck (Wheaton, Illinois: Victor Books, 1983), p. 654.

26. Walvoord, p. 143.

27. Lightner, p. 654.

28. J. I. Packer, *Knowing God* (Downers Grove, Illinois: InterVarsity Press, 1979), p. 50.

29. Louis Berkhof; cited by Gromacki, p. 106.

30. Gromacki, p. 107.

31. Gromacki, p. 110.

32. See Reymond, p. 79.

33. Gromacki, p. 106.

34. Walvoord, p. 115.

35. Robert P. Lightner, *Evangelical Theology* (Grand Rapids, Michigan: Baker Book House, 1986), p. 82.

36. Walvoord, p. 115.

37. Ryrie, p. 250.

38. Walvoord, p. 116.

39. See Gromacki, p. 109; and Walvoord, p. 115.

40. Walvoord, p. 118.

41. William G. T. Shedd; cited in Gromacki, p. 111

42. Reymond, p. 80.

Chapter 6—The Miracles of Jesus

1. Charles C. Ryrie, *The Miracles of Our Lord* (Neptune, New Jersey: Loizeaux Brothers, 1988), p. 16.

2. Those interested in understanding the hard sayings of Jesus can consult my book *What Did Jesus Mean? Making Sense of the Difficult Sayings of Jesus* (Eugene, Oregon: Harvest House Publishers, 1999).

3. William L. Lane, *The Gospel According to Mark* (Grand Rapids, Michigan: Eerdmans Publishing Company, 1974), p. 204.

4. Leon Morris, *Luke* (Grand Rapids, Michigan: Eerdmans Publishing Company, 1983), p 159.

5. *The Wycliffe Bible Commentary*, eds. Everett F. Harrison and Charles F Pfeiffer (Chicago, Illinois: Moody Press, 1974), p. 1048.

6. Peter H. Davids, *More Hard Sayings of the New Testament* (Downers Grove, Illinois: InterVarsity Press, 1991), p. 26.

7. Alfred Edersheim, cited in J. Dwight Pentecost, *The Words and Works of Jesus Christ* (Grand Rapids, Michigan: Zondervan Publishing House, 1981), p. 148.

Chapter 7—Miracles of the New Testament Apostles

1. *Zondervan NIV Bible Commentary*, eds. Kenneth L. Barker and John Kohlenberger III (Grand Rapids, Michigan: Zondervan Publishing House, 1994), p. 699.

2. *Expositor's Bible Commentary*, ed. Arno C. Gaebelein (Grand Rapids, Michigan: Zondervan Publishing House), Accordance Bible Software, electronic media.

3. F. F. Bruce, *The Book of Acts* (Grand Rapids, Michigan: Eerdmans Publishing Company, 1986), Acts 14:12.

4. *The Bible Knowledge Commentary*, New Testament, eds. John F. Walvoord and Roy Zuck (Wheaton, Illinois: Victor Books, 1983), p. 391.

Chapter 8—The New Testament Miracles of Miracles: the Resurrection

1. Cited in Tim LaHaye, *Jesus: Who Is He?* (Sisters, Oregon: Multnomah Books, 1996), p. 150.

2. *Evangelical Dictionary of Theology*, ed. Walter A. Elwell (Grand Rapids, Michigan: Baker Book House, 1984), p. 724.

3. Henry Clarence Thiessen, *Lectures in Systematic Theology* (Grand Rapids, Michigan: Eerdmans Publishing Company, 1979), p. 13.

4. Nancy Gibbs, "The Message of Miracles: Religious Controversy Over Validity of Miracles," *Time*, April 10, 1995, p. 64, Gale Group Magazine, downloaded from DIALOG database.

5. Gibbs, p. 64.

6. Robert Gundry, *Soma in Biblical Theology* (Cambridge, Massachusetts: Cambridge University Press, 1976), p. 168.

7. Canon Westcott, *The Gospel of the Resurrection*, Bible Illustrations, Logos Bible Software, electronic media.

8. Sir Edward Clarke; cited by John Stott, *Basic Christianity* (Downers Grove, Illinois: InterVarsity Press, 1971), p. 47.

9. Cited by Wilbur Smith, *Sermons on the Christian Life;* cited in Bible Illustrations, Logos Bible Software, electronic media.

Chapter 9—The Possibility of Miracles Today

1. Cited in Richard Mayhue, *The Healing Promise* (Eugene, Oregon: Harvest House Publishers, 1994), pp. 66-67.

2. John A. Witmer, "The Doctrine of Miracles," *Bibliotheca Sacra*, Logos Bible Software, electronic media.

3. *Evangelical Dictionary of Biblical Theology*, Logos Bible Software, electronic media.

4. Ken Boa and Larry Moody, *I'm Glad You Asked* (Wheaton, Illinois: Victor Books, 1994), p. 52.

5. James Oliver Buswell, *A Systematic Theology of the Christian Religion* (Grand Rapids, Michigan: Zondervan Publishing House, 1979), p. 180.

6. Douglas Connelly, *Miracles: What the Bible Says* (Downers Grove, Illinois: InterVarsity Press, 1997), p. 29.

7. Connelly, p. 46.

8. Jackie Deere, *Surprised by the Spirit* (Grand Rapids, Michigan: Zondervan, 1993), p. 74.

9. *The New Unger's Bible Dictionary* (Chicago, Illinois: Moody Press, 1988), PC Study Bible, electronic media.

10. Henry Clarence Thiessen, *Lectures in Systematic Theology* (Grand Rapids, Michigan: Eerdmans Publishing Company, 1979), p. 13.

11. Gordon Clark, "Miracles," *Zondervan Pictorial Encyclopedia of the Bible*, ed. Merrill C. Tenney (Grand Rapids, Michigan: Zondervan Publishing House, 1978), p. 249.

12. *Wycliffe Bible Encyclopedia*, The Word Processor, Bible Research Systems, electronic media.

13. R.C. Sproul, *Now, That's a Good Question* (Wheaton, Illinois: Tyndale House Publishers, 1996), p. 22.

14. Henry Morris, "Biblical Naturalism and Modern Science," *Bibliotheca Sacra*, Logos Bible Software, electronic media.

15. Witmer, "The Doctrine of Miracles."

16. Leon Morris, *The Gospel According to John* (Grand Rapids, Michigan: Eerdmans Publishing Company, 1987), p. 646.

17. *The IVP Bible Background Commentary,* New Testament, Logos Bible Software, electronic media.

18. *Wycliffe Bible Commentary,* The Word Processor, Bible Research Systems, electronic media.

19. David O'Brien, *Today's Handbook for Solving Bible Difficulties* (Minneapolis, Minnesota: Bethany House Publishers, 1990), p. 139.

20. Norman Geisler and Ron Rhodes, *When Cultists Ask* (Grand Rapids, Michigan: Baker Book House, 1997), p. 137.

21. Geisler and Rhodes, p. 137.

22. Norman L. Geisler, *Encyclopedia of Apologetics* (Grand Rapids, Michigan: Baker Book House, 1999), p. 470.

23. Geisler, p. 470.

24. Chuck Swindoll; cited in Mayhue, pp. 36-37.

25. James Oliver Buswell, *A Systematic Theology of the Christian Religion* (Grand Rapids, Michigan: Zondervan Publishing House, 1979), p. 180-81.

26. *Wycliffe Bible Encyclopedia,* The Word Processor.

27. J. I. Packer, "The Comfort of Conservativism," in *Power Religion,* ed. Michael Horton (Chicago, Illinois: Moody Press, 1992), p. 289.

Chapter 10—The Case Against Miracles

1. Gordon R. Lewis and Bruce A. Demerest, *Integrative Theology* (Grand Rapids, Michigan: Zondervan Publishing House, 1996), p. 75.

2. Lewis and Demerest, p. 75.

3. Norman L. Geisler, *The Battle for the Resurrection* (Nashville, Tennessee: Thomas Nelson Publishers, 1992), pp. 68-69.

4. Jodie Berndt, *Celebration of Miracles* (Nashville, Tennessee: Thomas Nelson Publishers, 1995), p. 20.

5. "Religious Doctrines and Dogmas: In the 18th and early 19th centuries," *Encyclopedia Britannica,* electronic media.

6. Cited in R. Douglas Geivett and Gary R. Habermas, *In Defense of Miracles: A Comprehensive Case for God's Action in History* (Downers Grove, Illinois: InterVarsity Press, 1997), p. 33.

7. John A. Witmer, "The Doctrine of Miracles," *Bibliotheca Sacra,* Logos Bible Software, electronic media.

8. One must recognize that the "laws" of science are generalizations based on repeated, testable experience. They are provisional to the extent that they are open to modification and correction in the light of further understanding.

9. Louis Berkhof, *Systematic Theology* (Grand Rapids, Michigan: Eerdmans Publishing Company, 1982), p. 177.

10. Charles Ryrie, *Survey of Bible Doctrine,* QuickVerse Library, electronic media.

11. Berkhof, p. 177.

12. Norman L. Geisler and Ronald M. Brooks, *When Skeptics Ask* (Wheaton, Illinois: Victor Press, 1989), p. 76.

13. Geisler and Brooks, p. 76.

14. Ken Boa and Larry Moody, *I'm Glad You Asked* (Wheaton, Illinois: Victor Books, 1994), pp. 50-51.

15. Boa and Moody, p. 53.

16. Peter Kreeft and Ronald Tacelli, *Handbook of Christian Apologetics* (Downers Grove, Illinois: InterVarsity Press, 1994), p. 109.

17. Cited in Geivett and Habermas, p. 33.

18. Norman Geisler, cited in Geivett and Habermas, p. 78.

19. Henry Clarence Thiessen, *Lectures in Systematic Theology* (Grand Rapids, Michigan: Eerdmans Publishing Company, 1979), p. 12.

20. Geisler and Brooks, pp. 79-80.

21. James Oliver Buswell, *A Systematic Theology of the Christian Religion* (Grand Rapids, Michigan: Zondervan Publishing House, 1979), p. 176.

22. C.S. Lewis, *God in the Dock* (Grand Rapids, Michigan: Eerdmans Publishing Company, 1972), p. 26.

23. Lewis, p. 26.

24. Ron Rhodes, *The Complete Book of Bible Answers* (Eugene, Oregon: Harvest House Publishers, 1999), p. 304.

25. Josh McDowell and Don Stewart, *Answers to Tough Questions* (Nashville, Tennessee: Thomas Nelson Publishers, 1993), p. 84.

26. Paul E. Little, *Know Why You Believe* (Downers Grove, Illinois: InterVarsity Press, 1975), p. 59.

27. Charles Hodge, *Systematic Theology*, Logos Bible Software, electronic media, insert added.

28. Norman L. Geisler, *Encyclopedia of Apologetics* (Grand Rapids, Michigan: Baker Book House, 1999), p. 450.

Chapter 11—Counterfeit Miracles

1. Ron Rhodes and Paul Carden, "What's New in the Headlines," *Christian Research Newsletter,* March/April 1992, p. 3.

2. Douglas Connelly, *Miracles: What the Bible Says* (Downers Grove, Illinois: InterVarsity Press, 1997), p. 14.

3. Connelly, p. 13.

4. See Dean C. Halverson, "A Course in Miracles: Seeing Yourself as Sinless," *SCP Journal* 7, 1 (1987): pp.18-27.

5. Tal Brooke, "The Cosmic Christ of Channeled Revelation," in *The Conspiracy to Silence the Son of God* (Eugene, Oregon: Harvest House Publishers, 1998), pp. 97-112.

6. David Gershon and Gail Straub, *Empowerment: The Art of Creating Your Life As You Want It* (New York, New York: Delta, 1989), p. 5.

7. Gershon and Straub, p. 21.

8. Gershon and Straub, p. 35.

9. Gershon and Straub, p. 36.

10. Gershon and Straub, p. 36.

11. Gershon and Straub, p. 200.

12. Gershon and Straub, p. 199.

13. Gershon and Straub, p. 199.

14. Gershon and Straub, p. 200.

15. Gershon and Straub, p. 36.

16. Shirley MacLaine, *Dancing in the Light* (New York, New York: Bantam, 1985), p. 133.

17. George Trevelyan, *Operation Redemption* (Walpole, New Hampshire: Stillpoint Publishing, 1981), p. 83.

18. Levi Dowling, *The Aquarian Gospel of Jesus the Christ* (London: L.N. Fowler & Co., 1947), p 126.

19. Dowling, p. 15.

20. Dowling, p. 263.

21. Norman L. Geisler and Ronald M. Brooks, *Christianity Under Attack* (Dallas, Texas: Quest Publications, 1985), p. 43.

22. Norman L. Geisler and Jeff Amano, *The Infiltration of the New Age* (Wheaton, Illinois: Tyndale House, 1989), p. 20.

23. According to New Thought, human beings can experience health, success, and abundant life by using their thoughts to define the condition of their lives. New Thought proponents subscribe to the "law of attraction." This law says that just as *like attracts like*, so our thoughts can attract the things they want or expect. Negative thoughts are believed to attract dismal circumstances; positive thoughts attract more desirable circumstances. Our thoughts can be either creative or destructive. New Thought sets out to teach people how to use their thoughts creatively. And Word-Faith teachers have adapted this methodology for their health-and-wealth gospel.

24. Kenneth Hagin, quoted in D. R. McConnell, *A Different Gospel* (Peabody, Massachusetts: Hendrickson Publishers, 1988), p. 175.

25. Robert Tilton, *Success-N-Life* television program (December 27, 1990).

26. Frederick Price, *Ever Increasing Faith* program on TBN (December 9, 1990).

27. John Avanzini, *Believer's Voice of Victory* program on TBN (January 20, 1991)

28. Avanzini, *Believer's Voice of Victory*.

29. John Avanzini, *Praise the Lord* program on TBN (September 15, 1988).

30. Kenneth Copeland, cited in McConnell, p. 171.

31. Marilyn Hickey; see Hank Hanegraaff, *Christianity in Crisis* (Eugene, Oregon: Harvest House Publishers, 1993), pp. 31, 36, 63, 79, 203, 207, 238, 249, 351-52, 417.

32. Kenneth Copeland, cited in McConnell, p. 172.

33. Kenneth Copeland, *Laws of Prosperity* (Fort Worth, Texas: Kenneth Copeland Publications, 1974), p. 67.

34. See Hanegraaff.

35. Connelly, p. 15.

36. Elliot Miller and Ken Samples, *The Cult of the Virgin* (Grand Rapids, Michigan: Baker Book House, 1992), pp. 107-8.

37. Ken Samples wrote a series of articles on Marian apparitions for the *Christian Research Journal* in which he pointed out these possible explanations for what people are experiencing.

38. Miller and Samples, pp. 107-8.

Chapter 12—Can the Devil Perform Miracles?

1. Charles C. Ryrie, *Balancing the Christian Life* (Chicago, Illinois: Moody Press, 1978), p. 124

2. Charles C. Ryrie, *A Survey of Bible Doctrine* (Chicago, Illinois: Moody Press, 1980), p. 94.

3. Charles C. Ryrie, *Basic Theology* (Wheaton, Illinois: Victor Books, 1986), p. 147.

4. Ryrie, *Balancing the Christian Life*, p. 124.

5. Merrill F. Unger, *Demons in the World Today* (Wheaton, Illinois: Tyndale House Publishers, 1972), p. 28.

6. Millard J. Erickson, *Christian Theology* (Grand Rapids, Michigan: Baker Book House, 1987), p. 450.

7. Ryrie, *Basic Theology*, p. 159, insert mine; see also Unger, *Demons in the World Today*, pp. 15-16.

8. See Ryrie, *Basic Theology*, p. 159.

9. Paul Enns, *The Moody Handbook of Theology* (Chicago, Illinois: Moody Press, 1989), p. 297.

10. Henry Morris, "Biblical Naturalism and Modern Science," *Bibliotheca Sacra*, Logos Bible Software, electronic media.

11. John A. Witmer, "The Doctrine of Miracles," *Bibliotheca Sacra*, Logos Bible Software, electronic media.

12. Charles Hodge, *Systematic Theology*, Logos Bible Software, electronic media, emphasis added.

13. Norman L. Geisler; cited in *Miracles Are Heaven Sent* (Tulsa, Oklahoma: Honor Books, 1995), p. 10.

14. Charles Hodge, *Systematic Theology*.

15. Geisler; cited in *Miracles Are Heaven Sent*, p. 10.

Chapter 13—Miracles of New Age "Energetic Medicine"

1. John Ankerberg and John Weldon, *The Facts on Holistic Health and New Age Medicine* (Eugene, Oregon: Harvest House Publishers, 1992), p. 5.

2. Sharon Begley, "Helping Docs Mind the Body," *Newsweek*, March 8, 1993, p. 61.

3. "Many Christians Found to Hold New Age Beliefs," *Los Angeles Times*, January 4, 1992, p. F23.

4. Rick Fields et al., eds., *Chop Wood, Carry Water* (Los Angeles, California: J. P. Tarcher, 1984), p. 186.

5. Ron Rhodes, *The New Age Movement* (Grand Rapids, Michigan: Zondervan Publishing House, 1996).

6. John Thie, *Touch for Health* (Marina del Rey, California: DeVorss, 1973).

7. See the Christian Chiropractors Association's "Policy Statement on New Age Healing" (CCA, 3200 S. Lemay Ave., Fort Collins, Colorado 80525-3605).

8. David Van Biema, "Emperor of the Soul Combining Medical Advice With Indian Metaphysics," *Time*, June 24, 1996, p. 64.

9. Andrew Weil, *Natural Health, Natural Medicine: A Comprehensive Manual for Wellness and Self-Care* (Boston, Massachusetts: Houghton Mifflin Company, 1990), p. 165.

10. Bernie Siegel, *Peace, Love & Healing* (New York, New York: Harper & Row Publishers, 1989), p. 247.

11 Bernie Siegel, *Love, Medicine & Miracles* (New York, New York: Harper & Row Publishers, 1986). p. 179.

12. Siegel, *Love, Medicine & Miracles*, p. 177.

13. Cited by Clete Hux, *The New Age Medicine of Dr. Bernie Siegel*, 1995, Watchman Fellowship Web Site, p. 252.

14. Siegel, *Love, Medicine & Miracles*, p. 254.

15. Hux.

16. Ron Rhodes, "Bernie Siegel, Healing, and Miracles," *Christian Research Newsletter*.

17. Biema, p. 64.

18. Deepak Chopra, *Ageless Body, Timeless Mind* (New York, New York: Harmony Books, 1993), p. 45, insert added.

19. Chopra, pp. 261-62

20. Chopra, p. 16.

21. Chopra, p. 264.

22. John Weldon and Stephen C. Myers, "A Summary Critique," *Christian Research Journal*, Winter 1994, p. 43.

23. Chip Brown, "Deepak Chopra   s (Sniff) a Cold," *Esquire*, October 1, 1995, p. 118.

24. Chopra, p. 6.

25. Deepak Chopra, *Perfect Health: The Complete Mind/Body Guide* (New York, New York: Harmony Books, 1990), p. 6.

26. Chopra, *Ageless Body, Timeless Mind*, p. 5.

27. Deepak Chopra. *Quantum Healing: Exploring the Frontiers of Mind/Body Medicine* (New York, New York: Bantam Books, 1989), p. 2.

28. Doug Levy, "Deepak Chopra's Path Toward an 'Ageless Body,'" *USA Today*, July 6, 1994, p. 1.

29. Chopra, *Ageless Body, Timeless Mind*, p. 6.

30. Chopra, *Ageless Body, Timeless Mind*, p. 6.

31. Chopra, *Ageless Body, Timeless Mind*, p. 6.

32. Douglas Groothuis, *Unmasking the New Age* (Downers Grove, Illinois: InterVarsity Press, 1986), p. 66.

33. Weil, *Natural Health, Natural Medicine*, p. 56.

34. Rhodes, "Bernie Siegel, Healing, and Miracles," *Christian Research Newsletter.*

35. Elliot Miller, "The Christian, Energetic Medicine, and 'New Age Paranoia,'" *Christian Research Journal*, Winter 1992, p. 26.

36. Miller, p. 26.

37. Siegel, *Love, Medicine & Miracles*, pp. 19-20.

38. Cathy Hainer, "An Alternative Prescription for Health," *USA Today*, March 26, 1997, p. 01D.

39. Weil, pp. 124-25.

40. John Weldon and John Ankerberg, "Visualization: God-Given Power or New Age Danger?" Part 1, *Christian Research Journal*, Summer 1996, p. 27. Note that eastern meditation should be distinguished from biblical meditation. Scripture defines meditation as the individual believer objectively contemplating and deeply reflecting upon God and His Word (Psalm 1:2; 19:14; Joshua 1:8) as well as His Person and faithfulness (Psalm 119; compare with 19:14; 48:9; 77:12; 104:34; 143:5). There is no subjective emptying of the mind in biblical meditation.

    Christian meditation calls us to look upward to God so that our minds may be filled with godly wisdom and insight, and so that our hearts may be filled with comfort, happiness, and joy. To echo the opening words of the psalmist, "Blessed is the man... [whose] delight is in the law of the LORD, and on his law he meditates day and night" (Psalm 1:1,2).

41. Weldon and Ankerberg, "Visualization," p. 21.

42. Miller, p. 27.

43. Groothuis, p. 67.

44. *The Christian Belief in Divine Healing*, Watchman Fellowship Web Site, 1997.

Chapter 14—If Your Miracle Doesn't Come...

1. John Wesley, *The Nature of Spiritual Growth* (Minneapolis, Minnesota: Bethany House Publishers, 1987), p. 33.

2. A. W. Tozer, *The Pursuit of God* (Wheaton, Illinois: Tyndale House Publishers, n.d.), p. 56.

3. John Calvin, *Institutes of the Christian Religion*, ed. John T. McNeill, trans. Ford Lewis Battles (Philadelphia, Pennsylvania: Westminster, 1960), p. 548.

4. Calvin, p. 549.

5. George Müller, *Autobiography of George Müller: The Life of Trust* (Grand Rapids, Michigan: Baker Book House, 1984), p. 8.

6. Müller, p. 8.

7. Adrian Rogers, *Believe in Miracles but Trust in Jesus* (Wheaton, Illinois: Crossway Books, 1997), p. 13.

8. J. I. Packer, ed. *Alive to God: Studies in Spirituality* (Downers Grove, Illinois: InterVarsity Press, 1992), p. 162.

9. Packer, p. 171.

10. Packer, p. 171.

11. Packer, p. 163.

12. Packer, p. 164.

13. Packer, p. 165.

14. Packer, p. 165.

15. Richard Baxter; cited in Packer, p. 167.

16. Gary R. Habermas and J. P. Moreland, *Immortality: The Other Side of Death* (Nashville, Tennessee: Thomas Nelson Publishers, 1992), p. 185.

17. Habermas and Moreland, p. 186.

18. Calvin, p. 590.

19. Wesley, p. 189.

20. Charles Spurgeon; cited by Jim Elliot, *Shadow of the Almighty* (Grand Rapids, Michigan: Zondervan Publishing House, 1970), p. 83.

Appendix—The Miracle of a Changed Life

1. Adrian Rogers, *Believe in Miracles but Trust in Jesus* (Wheaton, Illinois: Crossway Books, 1997), p. 15.

2. Philip James Bailey, *Draper's Illustrations,* QuickVerse Library, Broderbund, electronic media.

3. Charles Hodge, *Systematic Theology,* Logos Bible Software, electronic media.

4. Leonard Ravenhill, *Draper's Illustrations,* QuickVerse Library, Broderbund, electronic media.

5. Henry Morris, "Biblical Naturalism and Modern Science," *Bibliotheca Sacra,* Logos Bible Software, electronic media.

Other Books by
Ron Rhodes

Alien Obsession
Examining the evidence behind alien visitations reveals their primary agenda—to change the way we think about God and His Word and to create a one-world religion. Rhodes explores the occult connection, the Roswell incident, and the Bible's view of extraterrestrials.

Angels Among Us
Angel sightings are recounted daily in talk shows, magazines, and newspapers. Why have angels suddenly become so popular? Discover just how much the Bible *does* say about angels, and how much of it applies to Christian living today.

The Complete Book of Bible Answers
This great resource addresses the difficult Bible questions that arise during Bible studies and witnessing—covering topics that range from the conflicts between science and the Bible to reconciling God's sovereignty with man's free will.

Reasoning from the Scriptures with the Mormons
Powerful tools for sharing the truth of God's Word in a loving and gracious way are presented in a simple, step-by-step format.

Reasoning from the Scriptures with the Jehovah's Witnesses
Many outstanding features make this the complete hands-on guide to sharing the truth of God's Word in a loving and gracious way. Includes favorite tactics used by the Witnesses and effective biblical responses.

What Did Jesus Mean?
Many people are perplexed over Christ's instructions to "pluck out an eye" or "let the dead bury the dead." This engaging book helps readers understand the first-century context and sheds light on its modern application.